Study Guide to Accompany Financial Accounting A User Perspective

Canadian Edition

Robert E. Hoskin
University of Connecticut

Dick Wasson
Southwestern College

Charlotte Heywood
Wilfrid Laurier University

John Wiley & Sons Canada, Ltd
• Toronto • New York • Chichester • Weinheim • Brisbane • Singapore

Canadian Cataloguing in Publication Data

Wasson, Dick
Study guide to accompany Financial accounting, a user perspective, first Canadian edition

ISBN 0-471-64213-4

1. Accounting - Problems, exercises, etc. I. Heywood, Charlotte. II. Hoskin, Robert E., 1949- . Financial accounting : a user perspective. III. Title.

HF5635.H85 1977 Suppl. 657'.044 C97-930429-6

Production Credits

Acquisitions Editor: John Horne
Publishing Services Director: Karen Bryan
Developmental Editor: Michael Schellenberg
Designer/Electronic Assembly: Vesna Mayer
Printing and Binding: Webcom Limited

Printed and Bound in Canada
10 9 8 7 6 5 4 3 2 1

TABLE OF CONTENTS

TO THE STUDENT

This study guide is designed for use with *Financial Accounting, A User Perspective*: A User Perspective, First Canadian Edition, by Robert E. Hoskin, Ronald A. Davidson, and Maureen R. Fizzell. It should not be used as a substitute for material presented in the textbook.

To assist you in the learning process, each chapter of this study guide contains the following components:

1. An overview of the chapter.
2. The learning objectives of the chapter.
3. A review of the chapter organized by learning objective and cross-referenced to the text.
4. Learning tips.
5. A self-study section that includes questions that test your understanding of key terms, assess your recall of concepts, and applying your knowledge.
6. Solutions to the self-study section.

Suggested Study Sequence

Learning accounting is similar to learning a foreign language. You must learn the vocabulary in order to learn how to use the language. As a result, a certain amount of memorization is necessary. However, the successful student will not rely solely on memorization. Instead, he or she will try to understand the conceptual basis for the principles presented in the text and then understand how to apply those principles. The following sequence represents one way that might be used to obtain that understanding.

1. Read each chapter **before** attending class. As you read, highlight the main ideas presented and make a list of the questions you have about the material. Take the list to class and make sure that you get an answer for each question.
2. Read the study guide, noting the learning tips and any cross-referenced material.
3. Reread the chapter, and work through the examples given to reinforce your understanding. Remember that reading alone is not studying so at this point you should outline the chapter and make notes about the material. The notes should not consist of passages copied from the text. As much as possible try to put them in your own words. Note any critical material discussed in the study guide.

4. Test your understanding of the material presented by attempting the self-study section in this guide. **Do not** look at the solutions until you have answered the questions.
5. If you cannot answer some of the questions correctly, reread the applicable section in the text and expand your notes.
6. Work the end-of-chapter items assigned by your instructor. You should continue to work problems until you not longer need to refer back to the text in order to do so. As one long-term accounting professor has told his students over and over again, "The only way to learn accounting is through the end of a pencil."

Good luck in your pursuit of the kinds of information that accounting can provide and the range of opportunity that it affords.

D. W.
C. W. H.

CHAPTER 1

OVERVIEW OF CORPORATE FINANCIAL ACCOUNTING

CHAPTER OVERVIEW

This opening chapter provides an overview of the types of activities business firms engage in and the contents of an annual report on the results of these activities. The typical activities of a firm are:

- operating activites
- investing activites, and
- financing activites.

An annual report normally contains the following:

- a Report to the Shareholders,
- a Corporate Profile,
- a List of the Board of Directors,
- the Financial Statements,
- Management's Discussion and Analysis,
- the Independent Auditors' Report, and
- the Notes to the Financial Statements.

In this chaper, the various users of a firm's annual report are identified and the professional bodies involved in developing the standards on which the financial statements are prepared are mentioned. Finally, the qualitative characteristics of accounting information are discussed.

Learning Objectives

1. Be aware of the predominant form of large business organization and its characteristics.
2. Be acquainted with who uses financial statements and why they use them.
3. Understand the importance of Generally Accepted Accounting Principles (GAAP), and identify the organizations that establish these principles.
4. Understand how the conceptual framework serves both a deductive and an inductive role in the development of accounting standards.
5. Be acquainted with the objectives of financial reporting.
6. Be familiar with the qualitative characteristics of accounting information.
7. Identify the types of activities that firms engage in and report on.
8. Understand the purpose and content of the Income Statement (Statement of Earnings).
9. Understand the purpose and content of the Balance Sheet (Statement of Financial Position).
10. Understand the purpose and content of the Statement of Changes in Financial Position (Cash Flows Statement).
11. Be familiar with the purpose and types of auditors' reports.

Chapter Review

1. Be aware of the predominant form of large business organization and its characteristics (p. 4)

The corporation is the predominant form of business organization for large businesses in Canada. The characteristics of a corporation include the following:

1. It is a separate legal entity from its owners.
2. The owners are the shareholders of the corporation.
3. The owners elect the Board of Directors.
4. The Board of Directors hires senior management.
5. Management provides periodic (quarterly and annual) reports to the owners.

2. Be acquainted with who uses financial statements and why they use them (pp. 4 and 7)

The users of the information contained in financial statements can be divided into two groups: internal users and external users.

Internal users focus on the information they find useful in making operational decisions. **External users** focus on the information they find useful in making investment and credit granting decisions.

Learning Tip

For a complete listing of the users within each of the two groups, see Exhibit 1-1 on page 5 of the text.

3. Understand the importance of Generally Accepted Accounting Principles (GAAP), and identify the organizations that establish these principles (pp. 7-10)

GAAP consists of the rules, concepts, and principles under which financial statements are prepared. In Canada, the Accounting Standards Board (AcSB) of the Canadian Institute of Chartered Accountants (CICA) sets accounting guidelines. These are published in the *CICA Handbook*. The current standard setting body in the United States is the Financial Accounting Standards Board (FASB).

4. Understand how the conceptual framework serves both a deductive and an inductive role in the development of accounting standards. (pp. 7-10)

The CICA has developed a set of objectives and concepts called the conceptual framework. This framework provides a foundation upon which the CICA can maintain a consistent approach in creating new accounting standards. The framework itself and the accounting standards derive from a political process of reaching consensus among the users of financial information.

5. Be acquainted with the objectives of financial reporting. (p. 7)

The conceptual framework defines the concepts of financial reporting and leads to the development of accounting guidelines from which financial statements are prepared. The objective is to provide information to external users which is useful to them in making decisions about the reporting entity.

The information that external users require in order to make rational decisions about the entity includes information about the resources of the entity and the claims against those resources, the changes that have occurred in those resources and the claims against them, and the results of the operations of the entity.

6. Be familiar with the qualitative characteristics of accounting information. (pp. 8-10)

According to Section 1000 of the *CICA Handbook*, accounting information should possess four qualitative characteristics. The purpose of identifying the characteristics is to provide the preparers of financial statements with a set of guidelines to use in evaluating the usefulness of information contained in the financial statements. The qualitative characteristics are defined below.

Understandibility: The user who is reasonably informed about business and economic activities should be able to understand the information.

Relevance: The information should make a difference in the decision-making of the user. The degree to which information is relevant to the user is governed by three factors: timeliness, predictive value, and feedback value. Accounting information should be **timely** if it is to be useful in decision making. Old information, like old news, may be interesting but it is of reduced relevance. Financial information should help the users increase their ability to **predict** the outcome of future events and should confirm or provide **feedback** to the users on their past predictions.

Reliability: The users should be able to accept the information and depend on it when making decisions. To be reliable the information must satisfy four criteria: representational faithfulness, verifiability, neutrality, and conservatism. **Representational faithfulness** means that the information is a faithful, or fair, representation of the facts or the events; that the substance of the event is described fairly.

Verifiabilty means the method of measurement has been applied without error. **Neutrality** means that the information is free of bias toward a particular outcome. **Conservatism** means that where there are two or more equally acceptable accounting alternatives, the alternative having the least favourable effect on net income is preferable.

Comparability means that reported information should be comparable among companies and consistent over time.

The constraints on the quality of reported information stress that the benefits of producing information should outweigh the costs of producing it (the **cost/benefit constraint**) and that strict adherence to accounting standards is not required for insignificant amounts (the **materiality constraint**).

Learning Tip

For a complete list of the characteristics of accounting information and their components, see Exhibit 1-2 on page 8 of the text.

7. Identify the types of activities that firms engage in and report on. (pp. 10-12)

The main activities of a business can be separated into three categories: financing activities, investing activities, and operating activities. **Financing activities** are those by which a firm obtains or repays funds (cash) and would include borrowing or issuing shares, repaying debt or repurchasing shares, and paying dividends. **Investing activities** are those in which a firm purchases property, plant, and equipment, invests in other corporations, sells property, plant and equipment, or sells its investments in other corporations. **Operating activities** relate to the normal, day-to-day activities of the firm in producing, marketing, and selling goods or services.

Learning Tip

For specific examples of each activity, see the shaded boxes on page 11 of the text.

8. Understand the purpose and content of the Income Statement (Statement of Earnings). (pp. 14-16)

The purpose of the Income Statement is to report the results of operations over a specific period of time. It reflects the resources flowing into the firm from the sale of its goods or services (revenues), and the resources flowing out of a firm for activities related to the generation of sales (expenses).

Learning Tip

The date line in the heading of the income statement will always read "For the year(s) ended December 31, 19XX."

In general, the statement contains headings identifying the name of the firm, the name of the statement, and the time period the statement covers; the revenues earned during the period; the expenses incurred; the net income or loss (the difference between the revenues and expenses); and the earnings per share (the net income or loss divided by the average number of common shares outstanding during the period).

Learning Tip

For an example of the form and content of the Income Statement see the shaded box on page 16 and BR-8 on page 61 of the text.

9. Understand the purpose and content of the Balance Sheet (Statement of Financial Position). (pp. 19-20)

The purpose of the Balance Sheet is to report the financial position of a firm at a point in time. The statement reflects the resources the firm owns (**assets**), the claims against those resources (**liabilities**), and the owners' interest in the firm (**owners' equity**).

Learning Tip

The date line in the heading of the Balance Sheet will always read "At December 31, 19XX."

The assets are listed in the order of their liquidity; that is, in the order of how quickly they can be turned into cash. In a classified balance sheet, the assets are divided into current and noncurrent categories. In an unclassified balance sheet no such distinction is made.

Learning Tip

For a list of common balance sheets assets see the shaded box on page 17 of the text.

Liabilities are usually reported in the order in which they will be paid. In a classified balance sheet, they are divided into current and noncurrent categories. In an unclassified balance sheet no such distinction is made.

Learning Tip

For a list of common balance sheet liabilities see the shaded box on page 18 of the text.

A measure of a firm's ability to meet its currently maturing debt is called working capital.

WORKING CAPITAL = CURRENT ASSETS – CURRENT LIABILITIES

Shareholders' (owners') equity includes the amount that the owners originally paid for their investment in shares of the corporation (share capital) plus the firm's accumulated earnings less accumulated dividends (retained earnings).

Learning Tip

For a list of common balance sheet shareholders' equity accounts see the shaded box on page 20 of the text.

The Statement of Financial Position is called the Balance Sheet because

ASSETS = LIABILITIES + SHAREHOLDERS' EQUITY

The equation can be rearranged to show that the shareholders' interest in the firm is represented by the firms' net assets, or assets minus liabilities.

SHAREHOLDERS' EQUITY = ASSETS – LIABILITIES

For a complete example of a Balance Sheet see BR-7 on page 60 of the text.

10. Understand the purpose and content of the Statement of Changes in Financial Position (Cash Flows Statement). (pp. 20-22)

The purpose of the Statement of Changes in Financial Position is to help investors, creditors, and other users in the following ways:

- to assess the past performance of the entity in generating and controlling cash resources;
- to assess the entity's probable future cash inflows, outflows, and net cash flows.

Learning Tip

The date line of the statement will always read "For the year(s) ended December 31, 19XX."

The Statement of Changes in Financial Position includes the following classifications:

Cash flows from operating activities—the net amount of cash generated or used in selling goods and providing services.

Cash flows from investing activities—the net amount of cash generated or used through sales and acquisistions of noncurrent assets.

Cash flows from financing activities—the net amount of cash generated or used through the issuance of long-term debt or share capital and the redemption of long-term debt or share capital.

Reconciling balances—the change in cash during the period.

Learning Tip

For a complete example of the Statement of Changes in Financial Position see BR-9 on page 62 of the text.

11. Be familiar with the purpose and types of auditors' reports. (pp. 25-26)

The purpose of the auditors' report is to provide the statement reader with an independent, professional opinion as to whether the financial statements are presented fairly in conformity with generally accepted accounting principles.

The types of reports (opinions) that can be issued include **an unqualified opinion**, **a qualified opinion**, **an adverse opinion**, and **a denial of opinion**.

Learning Tip

The financial statements are prepared by the firm's management, not the auditors. The auditors conduct an examination (audit) of the financial statements in order to express an opinion on the fairness of those statements.

SELF STUDY

MATCHING

Match the key term to the best explanation.

Key Terms

A. Assets
B. Balance sheet
C. Basic accounting equation
D. Expenses
E. AcSB
F. Financing activities
G. Income statement
H. Investing activities
I. Liability
J. Net income
K. Operating activities
L. Shareholders' equity
M. Retained earnings
N. Revenues
O. Statement of Changes in Financial Position

Explanations

1. M Earnings that the firm does not pay out to the owners in the form of dividends.
2. I Requires a probable future sacrifice of resources.
3. B Represents the financial position of the firm at a particular point in time.
4. J Revenues minus expenses.
5. L Consists of share capital and retained earnings.
6. K Activities involving the production and sale of a firm's goods and services.
7. E The current rule setting body of accounting standards.
8. N Inflow of resources from the sale of goods and services.
9. F Activities that raise funds (cash) with which the firm can operate.
10. O A statement that describes the inflows and outflows of cash during a specific time period.
11. D Resources flowing out of the firm related to the production of revenues.
12. C Assets = Liabilities + Shareholders' Equity
13. A Items a firm owns or has the right to use and that have probable future value.
14. H Activities involving the purchase of noncurrent assets.
15. G Discloses the results of operations for a specific period of time.

ASSESS YOUR RECALL

1. Identify the three types of activities that all firms engage in and give two examples of each activity.

FINANCIAL Activities:
- borrowing $
- issuing shares

OPERATING Activities:
- selling goods + services
- marketing

INVESTING Activities:
- buying plant + equipment
- investing in other companies

2. List four types of auditors' reports.

an unqualified opinion
a qualified opinion
an adverse opinion
a denial of opinion

3. Identify the four qualitative characteristics of accounting information.

understandability
relevance
reliability
comparability

APPLYING YOUR KNOWLEDGE

1. Given the following information taken from the financial records of Danforth Co. Ltd., calculate the balance in retained earnings as at December 31, 19X2.

Retained Earnings, December 31, Year 1	$ 80,000	Dividends Declared	$ 6,500
Share Capital	33,000	Operating Expenses	33,000
Revenues	150,000	Cost of Goods Sold	45,000

2. Given the following information from the financial records of Zaira, Inc. as of December 31, 19X1.

Accounts Payable	$ 16,000	Note Payable (due 2/1/19X3)	$ 40,000
Accounts Receivable	29,000		
Cash	22,000		
Share Capital	84,000	Prepaid Expenses	7,000
Intangible Assets	25,000	Capital Assets	51,000
Inventory	62,000		
Note Payable		Retained Earnings	25,000
(due 6/30/19X2)	12,000	Taxes Payable	17,000
		Dividends Payable	2,000

a. Prepare a classified balance sheet.

b. Determine the amount of working capital (show all calculations):

3. Given the following information from the books of Nordic Equipment Limited for the year ended December 31, 19X1, prepare an income statement:

Accounts Payable	$ 30,000	Other Expenses	$ 2,000
Cash	25,000	Other Income	7,000
Share Capital		Prepaid Expenses	12,000
(10,000 shares)	100,000	Retained Earnings	25,000
Cost of Goods Sold	75,000	Sales Revenue	120,000
Dividends Declared	5,000	Tax Expense	10,000
Operating Expenses	20,000		

4. Indicate whether each of the following transactions is an operating (O), investing (I), or financing (F) activity:

1. O Collection of accounts receivable
2. F Repayment of a loan
3. F Repurchase of shares
4. I Sale of the investment in shares of another company
5. O Payment of accounts payable
6. O Sales to customers
7. I Sale of equipment
8. F Issuing shares
9. O Payment of taxes
10. F Payment of dividends

SOLUTIONS TO CHAPTER 1

MATCHING

1.	M	6.	K	11.	D
2.	I	7.	E	12.	C
3.	B	8.	N	13.	A
4.	J	9.	F	14.	H
5.	L	10.	O	15.	G

ASSESS YOUR RECALL

1. *Financing Activities:*

Borrowing money
Repaying loans
Issuing shares
Redemption of share capital
Paying dividends on shares

Investing Activities:

Purchase of equipment
Sale of a building
Investments in the shares of other companies
Sale of investments in shares of other companies

Operating Activities:

Sales to customers
Collections on accounts receivable
Purchase of inventory
Payments on accounts payable
Payment of operating expenses
Payment of tax expense

2. *Types of Audit Reports*
   Unqualified opinion
   Qualified opinion
   Adverse opinion
   Denial of opinion

3. The qualitative characteristics of accounting information are understandibility, relevance, reliability, and comparability.

APPLYING YOUR KNOWLEDGE

1.

Revenues	$150,000
Less:	
Cost of Goods Sold	45,000
Operating expenses	33,000
	78,000
Net income	$ 72,000

Retained Earnings,	
Dec. 31, 19X1	$ 80,000
Net income	72,000
Dividends Declared	(6,500)
Retained Earnings,	
Dec. 31, 19X2	$ 145,500

2. a.

Zaira, Inc.
Balance Sheet
At December 31, 19X1

ASSETS	
Current Assets	
Cash	$22,000
Accounts Receivable	29,000
Inventory	62,000
Prepaid Expenses	7,000
Total Current Assets	120,000
Capital Assets	51,000
Intangible Assets	25,000
Total Assets	$196,000
LIABILITIES AND SHAREHOLDERS' EQUITY	
Current Liabilities	
Accounts Payable	$16,000
Note Payable (due 6/30/19X2)	12,000
Dividends Payable	2,000
Taxes Payable	17,000
Total Current Liabilities	47,000
Long-term Note Payable (due 2/1/19X3)	40,000
Shareholders' Equity	
Share Capital	84,000
Retained Earnings	25,000
Total Shareholders' Equity	109,000
Total Liabilities & Shareholders' Equity	$196,000

b. Working capital = \$120,000 − 47,000 = \$73,000

3.

Nordic Equipment Limited
Income Statement
For the Year Ended December 31, 19X1

Revenues	
Sales Revenue	\$120,000
Other Income	7,000
Total Revenues	127,000
Costs and Expenses	
Cost of Goods Sold	75,000
Operating Expenses	20,000
Other Expenses	2,000
Total Costs and Expenses	97,000
Income Before Income Taxes	30,000
Income Tax Expense	10,000
Net Income	\$20,000
Earnings Per Share	\$2.00

Note: Earnings Per Share = \$20,000/10,000 shares

4.

1. O
2. F
3. F
4. I
5. O
6. O
7. I
8. F
9. O
10. F

CHAPTER 2

ACCOUNTING SYSTEMS

CHAPTER OVERVIEW

Chapter 1 detailed how a firm reports its profits (the income statement) and its financial position (the balance sheet). This chapter details how a firm collects, classifies, and aggregates the data necessary to prepare these statements. In order to understand this process, the basic accounting equation is used to illustrate the accounting for a firm's transactions and the preparation of its financial statements.

The chapter also continues the discussion of generally accepted accounting principles (GAAP) and accounting concepts as they apply to specific transactions for a retail company. Three measures of profitability are discussed. In addition, the format and content of the statement of cash flows is presented.

The basic concepts of the double entry system are illustrated including the meaning of the terms **debit** and **credit**. Illustrations are provided to show how transactions are analyzed and recorded in the books using accrual basis accounting. Finally, the steps in the accounting cycle are presented and discussed.

LEARNING OBJECTIVES

1. Understand how to analyze transactions using the basic accounting equation.
2. Understand the difference between cash basis and accrual basis accounting.
3. Understand the revenue recognition principle and the matching principle.
4. Understand the purpose and use of the cost principle.
5. Understand when it is necessary to recognize an expenditure as an asset.
6. Know how to calculate amortization.

7. Understand how and when to recognize interest.
8. Understand how to record the issuance of shares and the payment of dividends.
9. Understand how nonmonetary exchanges are valued.
10. Be familiar with several profitability measures.
11. Be familiar with the purpose and components of the statement of changes in financial position.
12. Be familiar with the purpose and components of the statement of retained earnings.
13. Understand how the double entry bookkeeping system works.
14. Be familiar with the components of the accounting cycle.

Chapter Review

1. Understand how to analyze transactions using the basic accounting equation. (pp. 79-96)

The basic accounting equation is the basis for analyzing and recording all transactions. It can be expressed as follows:

Assets = Liabilities + Shareholders' Equity or

A = L + SE

Note: At least two items are affected for each transaction in the equation; that is, the equality of the equation is always maintained.

2. Understand the difference between cash basis and accrual basis accounting. (pp. 86-87)

Cash basis accounting recognizes revenue from the sale of goods and services only when cash is received and recognizes expenses only when cash is paid out. This basis is used by some farmers, lawyers, and professional service organizations.

Accrual basis accounting recognizes revenue when it is earned and recognizes expenses when they are incurred regardless of when cash is received or paid out.

Learning Tip

Cash basis accounting measures performance only when cash is received or paid, while accrual basis accounting measures performance in the period in which the performance takes place.

3. Understand the revenue recognition principle and the matching principle. (pp. 86-88)

The revenue recognition criteria are necessary to ensure that revenues recognized under the accrual basis are reasonable (reliably measureable) and have a high probability of collectability (will result in cash inflows).

The matching principle is necessary in order to measure performance; that is, to match revenues and the cost of generating that revenue for a particular period of time (on the income statement). Expenses are recognized in the same period as the revenues that they helped to generate.

4. Understand the purpose and use of the cost principle. (pp. 88, 91, and 94)

Assets are initially recorded at their acquisition cost (historical cost). They are then reported at this same amount in the financial statements until they are sold or used.

Cost is used because it is more reliable and objective than estimates of an asset's value.

5. Understand when it is necessary to recognize an expenditure as an asset. (pp. 84-85)

The expenditure must meet the criteria for an asset: it must have probable future value and the company must either own it or have the right to use it.

The expenditure must be valued at its acquisition cost. In addition, the asset's useful life, how it will be used up over time, and its estimated residual value must be determined.

6. Know how to calculate amortization. (pp. 91-92)

Amortization is the systematic and rational allocation of the cost of a noncurrent asset over the asset's useful life. The most common method in use and the one illustrated in this chapter is straight-line amortization.

$$\text{Annual amortization} = \frac{\text{Original cost} - \text{Estimated Residual Value}}{\text{Estimated useful life}}$$

Learning Tip

The rationale for the amortization of certain assets is found in the matching principle which requires that expenses be matched to the revenues they helped to generate, period by period.

Amortization is a noncash expense. This is one reason why net income and the change in cash do not agree.

Land is an asset which is considered to have indefinite future benefit. As a result, amortization expense is never charged against this asset.

7. Understand how and when to recognize interest expense. (pp. 88, 89, and 93)

Interest expense is not recognized on accounts receivable or accounts payable. It is recognized only on notes receivable and notes payable.

When a firm receives a payment on a note receivable or makes a payment on a note payable, a portion of the payment represents repayment of the amount borrowed (**principal**); the remainder represents the cost of borrowing (**interest**). The principal payment reduces the amount of the note receivable or note payable while the interest is recognized as a revenue or an expense.

Learning Tip

Interest rates are generally quoted on an annual basis unless the terms of the loan specifically state otherwise.

The formula to calculate interest is as follows:

Interest = Principal x Interest Rate x Time

8. Understand how to record the issuance of shares and the payment of dividends. (pp. 93-95)

The sale of shares is recorded at fair market value on the date of sale. The selling price is recorded in the Share Capital account.

Dividends are payments to the shareholders of a firm—they are a return on the shareholders' investment in the company. They are declared by the firm's board of directors. A legal liability exists on the date that the dividend is declared (declaration date). The liability is satisfied when the firm makes payment.

Learning Tip

Dividends are not an expense so they do not appear on the income statement—they are recorded in the retained earnings account. However, payment of dividends does result in cash outflow which is reflected on the statement of changes in financial position. This is another reason why net income and the change in cash do not agree.

9. Understand how nonmonetary exchanges are valued. (p. 94)

Nonmonetary exchanges occur when two or more noncash items are exchanged; for example, a firm acquiring a piece of land in exchange for its common shares. The general rule is to value the item acquired at the value of the item given up.

10. Be familiar with several profitability measures. (p. 97)

Profitability ratios are used to measure a firm's profits in several ways. Chapter Two of the text introduces three alternatives:

- return on revenues,
- return on assets, and
- return on equity.

The profit margin ratio measures profitability in terms of revenues:

Profit Margin ratio = Net income/Revenues

The return on assets measures profitability in terms of the average assets invested in the firm:

$$\text{Return on Assets} = \frac{\text{Net income}}{\text{Average total assets}}$$

Average total assets is calculated by adding the total assets at the beginning of the period to the total assets at the end of the period and then dividing that sum by two.

The return on equity measures profitability in terms of the average total owners' equity:

$$\text{Return on Equity} = \frac{\text{Net income}}{\text{Average shareholders' equity}}$$

Average shareholders' equity is calculated by adding the balance of shareholders' equity at the beginning of the period to the balance at the end of the period and then dividing that sum by two.

Learning Tip

None of these measures is meaningful to the users of the financial statments unless the users compare the ratios over time within the firm and also among firms within the same industry.

11. Be familiar with the purpose and components of the statement of changes in financial position. (pp. 97-100)

The purpose of the statement of changes in financial position is to reflect the sources and uses of cash within a firm and the net change in cash during a period of time. The statement can be prepared using either the direct method or the indirect method.

The sources and uses of cash are linked to the types of business activities discussed in Chapter One; that is, operating activities, investing activities, and financing activities.

Operating cash flows come from:

- the sale of a firm's goods or services,
- the collections on those sales, and
- the expenses incurred to generate those sales.

Investing cash flows come from:

- the purchase and/or sale of investments, property, plant, and equipment, and
- the purchase and/or sale of other noncurrent assets.

Financing cash flows come from:

- the sale and/or repurchase of a firm's shares;
- the payment of dividends; and
- borrowings and repayments.

Learning Tip

For examples of the Statement of Changes in Financial Position see page 98 (direct method) and Exhibit 2-3 on page 99 (indirect method) of the text.

Analysis of the Statement of Changes in Financial Position should ask two questions. Is the cash flow from operating activities adequate to support the other activities? Which of the sources and uses of cash are recurring and which are infrequent?

12. Be familiar with the purpose and components of the statement of retained earnings. (p. 115)

The purpose of the statement of retained earnings is to show how the balance of retained earnings changed from one reporting period to the next. The two items that affect the account's balance are the net income/loss of the period and the dividends declared. Net income increases the account while a net loss and dividends declared decrease the account.

Learning Tip

For an example of the statement's format see Exhibit 2-18 on page 115 of the text.

To understand how net income/loss and dividends declared flow into the retained earnings account see Exhibit 2-17 on page 115 of the text.

13. Understand how the double entry bookkeeping system works. (pp. 100-104)

All accounts have a left side and a right side. The left side is called the debit

(DR) side, and the right side is called the credit (CR) side.

Recall the basic accounting equation where

Assets = Liabilities + Shareholders' Equity

and

Left = Right

or

Debit = Credit

Learning Tip

The effect on the accounts in the financial statements, how to increase and decrease them, and the normal balance in the account are outlined below:

Account	Increase	Decrease	Normal Balance
Assets	Debit	Credit	Debit
Liabilities	Credit	Debit	Credit
Owners' Equity	Credit	Debit	Credit
Revenues	Credit	Debit	Credit
Expenses	Debit	Credit	Debit
Dividends	Debit	Credit	Debit

Note that, in accounting, the terms debit (dr) and credit (cr) have no meaning other than left and right.

Each time a transaction occurs it is recorded by journal entry in the General Journal. Each journal entry consists of at least one debit and one credit; that is, at least two accounts are affected by each journal entry. The General Journal (and other specialized journals) are referred to as books of original entry.

Learning Tip

For each journal entry the equality of the accounting equation must be maintained; that is, the debits must always equal the credits.

The balances of asset, liability, and shareholders' equity accounts are carried over from one period to the next. These accounts are called permanent accounts.

The balances of revenue, expense, and dividends declared accounts are closed to retained earnings each period. These accounts are called temporary accounts. See Exhibit 2-7 on p. 103.

14. Be familiar with the components of the accounting cycle. (pp. 104-107)

The accounting cycle consists of a series of actions that relate to the recording and reporting of transactions and events within a firm during a period of time. These include the following:

a. Preparing a chart of accounts.
b. Entering the opening balances.
c. Determining if an accounting transactions or event has occurred.
d. Performing an analysis of the transaction.
e. Recording the transactions in the journal(s).
f. Posting the information from the journal(s) to the general ledger.
g. Preparimg a trial balance.
h. Preparing and posting the adjusting entries.
i. Preparing an adjusted trial balance.
j. Preparing the financial statements.
k. Preparing and posting the closing entries.

Learning Tip

The Chart of Accounts is a listing of accounts by name and number. The accounts are always kept in the same order: the permanent accounts; assets, liabilities, and shareholders' equity followed by the temporary accounts; revenues, expenses, and dividends. For an example, see Exhibit 2-9 on page 105 of the text.

For examples of journal entries, ledger accounts, and a trial balance see Exhibit 2-11 (p. 108) and Exhibits 2-12 and 2-13 (p. 109) of the text.

For examples of the closing journal entries see Exhibits 2-17 on page 115.

SELF STUDY

MATCHING

Match the key term to the best explanation.

Key Terms

A. Accrual basis
B. Adusting entry
C. Chart of accounts
D. Debit
E. Credit
F. Cost to be amortized
G. Amortization
H. Double entry accounting system
I. Journal
J. Ledger
K. Matching principle
L. Permanent accounts
M. Residual value
N. T-account
O. Trial balance

Explanations

1. _N_ A device used to represent a ledger account.
2. _E_ The right side of any account.
3. _L_ Balance sheet accounts.
4. _F_ The original cost of an asset less its estimated residual value.
5. _A_ The accounting basis that recognizes revenues and expenses in the period in which they are earned or incurred.
6. _I_ (crossed out; O in margin) A listing of account balances.
7. _B_ An entry made at the end of an accounting period to record an event or transaction that was not recorded during the period.
8. _K_ Requires that expenses related to the production of revenues be recognized in the same period as those revenues.
9. _H_ A system that requires that debits equal credits for each entry.
10. _D_ The left side of any account.
11. _M_ An estimate of an asset's value at the end of its useful life, made at the time of acquisition.
12. _C_ A listing of the accounts used in an accounting system.
13. _G_ A systematic, rational process of allocating the cost of a noncurrent asset over its useful life.
14. _I_ Where transactions and events are first recorded.
15. _O_ (crossed out; J in margin) Where transactions and events are summarized by account.

ASSESS YOUR RECALL

1. Complete the following matrix by indicating if an account is increased or decreased with debits or credits:

Type of Account	Debit	Credit
Asset	↑	↓
Liability	↓	↑
Owners' Equity	↓	↑
Revenue	↓	↑
Expense	↑	↓
Dividend Declared	↑	↓

2. List the accounting cycle steps that occur every accounting period, in the proper sequence.

1) Charts of Accounts
2) Opening Balances
3) Transactions or events
4) Transactions analysis
5) Journal entries
6) Post to Ledger
7) Trial Balance
8) Adjust Entries
9) Adjust Trial Balance
10) Prepare financial statements
11) Closing Entries

3. Indicate the accounts that are debited and credited in each of the following closing entries:

	Debit	Credit
a. To close the revenue account(s)	Revenue	Income Summary
b. To close the expense account(s)	Inc. Summary	Expense
c. To close the income summary	Inc. Summary	Retained Earnings
d. To close dividends declared	Retained Earnings	Dividends Declared

APPLYING YOUR KNOWLEDGE

1. Given the following data:

	19X4	19X3
Total assets	$ 22,500	$ 15,000
Total liabilities	9,000	4,500
Total shareholders' equity	13,500	10,500
Revenues	2,500	1,875
Expenses	2,125	1,725

a. Compute profit margin for 19X4:

b. Compute the return on assets for 19X4:

c. Compute the return on equity for 19X4:

2. Given the following trial balance for Vista, Inc. as of December 31, 19X4, prepare a statement of retained earnings:

	Debit	Credit
Current assets	$ 45,000	
Noncurrent assets	150,000	
Liabilities		$ 40,000
Issued capital		65,000
Retained earnings		75,000
Revenues		110,000
Expenses	94,000	
Dividends declared	1,000	
Totals	$ 290,000	$ 290,000

3. Karvel, Inc. began 19X4 with a $250,000 cash balance and ended the year with $360,800 in cash. During the year the following transactions occurred:

a. Issued common shares for $60,000.
b. Purchased equipment for $208,000.
c. Purchased merchandise inventory for $160,000 on account.
d. Borrowed $80,000 at 12% on July 1, interest payable semi-annually.
e. Sold inventory for $320,000, one-fourth of which were cash sales.
f. Paid employees $62,400.
g. Collected $224,000 on customers' accounts.
h. Paid suppliers $144,000.
i. Sold an investment in another company's shares for $100,000.
j. Received $6,000 of interest revenue from an investment.
k. Repurchased its own common shares from its investors for $20,000.
l. Paid semi-annual interest on the note payable.

Prepare a statement of changes in financial position for 19X4 using the direct method.

4. Prepare journal entries for the following transactions:

   a. Issued 10,000 shares for $25 a share.
   b. Exchanged 200 shares for equipment with an estimated useful life of 4 years and an estimated residual value of $400.
   c. Purchased $15,000 of inventory on credit.
   d. Purchased land for $150,000, one-third in cash and the balance on a 5-year, 12% note payable.
   e. Sold $10,000 of inventory for $18,000.
   f. Paid $5,000 for a 2-year insurance policy.
   g. Paid employee wages of $7,500.
   h. Received $8,000 from customers in payment of their accounts.
   i. Declared a $1,000 dividend.
   j. Paid suppliers $12,000 on account.
   k. Made a $32,000 payment on the note payable, $20,000 of which was a principal payment.
   l. Recognized one full year's amortization on the equipment.

	Debit	Credit

5. Given the following transactions:
   a. Issued shares for $250,000.
   b. Exchanged $5,000 of shares for equipment.
   c. Purchased $15,000 of inventory on credit.
   d. Sold $10,000 of inventory for $28,000.
   e. Paid employees $7,000.
   f. Received $8,000 from customers on account.
   g. Declared a $1,000 dividend.
   h. Paid suppliers $12,000 on account.
   i. Recognized $2,000 of amortization.

   Indicate the effect of these transactions on the accounting equation.

SOLUTIONS TO CHAPTER 2

MATCHING

1.	N	6.	O	11.	M
2.	E	7.	B	12.	C
3.	L	8.	K	13.	G
4.	F	9.	H	14.	I
5.	A	10.	D	15.	J

ASSESS YOUR RECALL

1.

Type of Account	Debit	Credit
Asset	Increase	Decrease
Liability	Decrease	Increase
Shareholders' Equity	Decrease	Increase
Revenue	Decrease	Increase
Expense	Increase	Decrease
Dividend Declared	Increase	Decrease

2.

Enter the beginning balances in the accounts.
Determine whether a transaction or event requiring accounting recognition has occurred.
Analyze the transaction or event.
Enter the transaction in the journal.
Post to the general ledger.
Prepare a trial balance.
Enter the adjusting entries in the journal and post to the general ledger.
Prepare an adjusted trial balance.
Prepare the financial statements.
Enter the closing entries in the journal and post to the general ledger.

3.

Debit	Credit
a. Revenue	Income Summary
b. Income Summary	Expense
c. Income Summary	Retained Earnings
d. Retained Earnings	Dividends Declared

APPLYING YOUR KNOWLEDGE

1.

a. Net income = revenues - expenses = 2,500 - 2,125 = 375
Profit margin = net income/ revenues
= 375/2,500
= 15%

b. Return on assets = net income/average assets
= 375/[(15,000 + 22,500)/2]
= 2%

c. Return on equity = net income/average shareholders' equity
= 375/[(10,500 + 13,500)/2]
= 3.125%

2.

Vista, Inc.
Statement of Retained Earnings
For the Year Ended December 31, 19X4

Retained earnings, December 31, 19X3	$ 75,000
Plus: Net income	16,000
Less: Dividends declared	1,000
Retained earnings, December 31, 19X4	$ 90,000

3.

Karvel, Inc.
Statement of Changes in Financial Position
For the Year Ended December 31, 19X4

Cash from operating activities:		
Cash sales	$ 80,000	
Collections from customers	224,000	
Interest from investment	6,000	
Payments to employees	(62,400)	
Payments to suppliers	(144,000)	
Payments for interest	(4,800)	
Cash provided by operating activities		$ 98,800
Cash from investing activities:		
Proceeds from sale of investment	100,000	
Purchase of equipment	(208,000)	
Cash used by investing activities		(108,000)
Cash from financing activities:		
Proceeds from issuance of shares	60,000	
Proceeds from note payable	80,000	

Repurchase of Karvel shares	(20,000)	
Cash provided by financing activities		120,000
Net increase in cash		110,800
Cash balance, December 31, 19X3		250,000
Cash balance, December 31, 19X4		$ 360,800

4.

	Debit	Credit
a. A—Cash	250,000	
SE—Common Shares		250,000
b. A—Equipment	5,000	
SE—Common Shares		5,000
c. A—Merchandise Inventory	15,000	
L—Accounts Payable		15,000
d. A—Land	150,000	
A—Cash		50,000
L—Notes Payable		100,000
e. A—Cash	18,000	
SE—Cost of Goods Sold	10,000	
SE—Revenue		18,000
A—Merchandise Inventory		10,000
f. A—Prepaid Insurance	5,000	
A—Cash		5,000
g. SE—Wages Expense	7,500	
A—Cash		7,500
h. A—Cash	8,000	
A—Accounts Receivable		8,000
i. SE—Dividends Declared	1,000	
L—Dividends Payable		1,000
j. L—Accounts Payable	12,000	
A—Cash		12,000
k. L—Notes Payable	20,000	
SE—Interest Expense	12,000	
A—Cash		32,000

l. SE—Amortization Expense	1,150	
A—Equipment		1,150

5. (Amounts in thousands)

Trans	+ Cash	+ A/R	+ Inv	+ Equip	=	+ A/P	Div + Pay	+ CS	+ CC	+ RE
a	++250							++100	++150	
b				++ 5				++ 2	++ 3	
c			++ 15			++ 15				
d	++ 28									++28
			+- 10							+- 10
e	+- 7									+- 7
f	++ 8	++ 8								
g							++ 1			+- 1
h	+- 12					+- 12				
i				+- 2						+- 2
Totals	+267	− 8	+ 5	+ 3	=	+ 3	+ 1	+ 102	+ 153	+ 8
Net				+267	=	+267				

CHAPTER 3

MANUFACTURING CORPORATIONS/FORMAT OF THE INCOME STATEMENT AND BALANCE SHEET

CHAPTER OVERVIEW

This chapter continues the discussion on financial statement format but from the perspective of a manufacturing firm. In addition, the discussion of adjusting journal entries is continued and the flow of information through the accounting system of a typical manufacturing entity is described. For example, a manufacturing firm maintains three separate inventory accounts—raw materials, work-in-process, and finished goods—unlike a merchandising firm which maintains only one inventory account. A major accounting concern in manufacturing firms is the proper valuation of the work-in-process and finished goods inventories. In order to capture the correct cost of these inventories, the firm's accounting system must differentiate between product costs and period costs.

The continuing discussion on journal entries includes a description of the proper accounting treatment of prepaid and accrued expenses as well as the recording and reporting of income tax expense.

In addition, this chapter expands on the previous discussions of the income statement and the balance sheet. The single-step format and the multistep format of the income statement are illustrated and described. Regardless of which income statement format is chosen by a firm, discontinued operations and extraordinary items should be disclosed separately and net of income taxes. Finally, the classified balance sheet and the unclassified balance sheet are illustrated and described.

LEARNING OBJECTIVES

1. Be able to define and give examples of product costs.
2. Be able to classify production costs.

3. Be able to describe the flow of production costs through a manufacturing firm.
4. Be able to calculate and to understand the significance of the Gross Profit Ratio and the Inventory Turnover Ratio.
5. Understand the significance of the information reported in the income statement.
6. Be able to describe and to illustrate the single-step and the multistep forms of the income statement.
7. Know and understand the basic elements of the income statement.
8. Have a firm understanding of the balance sheet elements and its common formats.
9. Be able to identify and account for accrued expenses.
10. Be able to identify and account for prepaid expenses.

CHAPTER REVIEW

1. Be able to define and give examples of product costs. (pp. 147-149)

Manufacturing firms purchase raw materials, convert them to finished products, and then sell them. Product costs are those costs incurred in the production of the finished product. They consist of direct costs and indirect costs.

Learning Tip

A direct cost is a cost that is directly and easily traceable to an inventory item. An indirect cost is one that is incurred in the production process but is not easily traceable to any particular inventory item.

2. Be able to classify production costs. (p. 149)

The three elements of production costs are direct materials, direct labour, and manufacturing overhead. Direct material costs are the costs of all materials directly and easily traceable to the finished product.

Direct labour costs are those labour costs incurred in transforming the direct materials into a finished product; that is, the "hands-on" labour costs. Manufacturing overhead costs include all other costs incurred in the production process. These include, for example, supplies, the salaries of factory supervisors, factory maintenance, factory amortization expense, and the cost of insuring production facilities. Manufacturing overhead costs are allocated on some reasonable basis to the manufactured product in finished goods inventory.

Learning Tips

Product costs are carried in the Work-In-Process and Finished Goods inventory accounts until the inventory is sold. The costs are then transferred to the Cost of Goods Sold account and become expenses.

All other costs incurred in running the firm such as selling and administrative costs are classified as period costs. Period costs are considered to relate to the passage of time and are expensed in the period in which they are incurred. Examples of period costs include executive salaries, the cost of the accounting department, and interest expense.

3. Be able to describe the flow of production costs through a manufacturing firm. (pp. 152–153)

As direct materials are removed from the Raw Materials inventory and put into production, the costs of those materials are transferred to Work-in-Process inventory.

As labour costs are incurred on the plant floor transforming the raw materials into finished product, the cost of that labour is charged to Work-in-Process inventory. Similarly, overhead costs incurred are allocated to the Work-in-Process inventory as production proceeds.

As products are completed, their allocated costs (materials, labour, and overhead) are transferred to Finished Goods inventory. The costs will remain in inventory until the goods are sold when they will be transferred to the Cost of Goods Sold expense account.

Learning Tip

Note that the cost of goods manufactured (COGM) represents the cost of completed goods transferred from the work-in-process inventory to the finished goods inventory. While these costs are in an inventory account they are assets. Only when the inventory is sold do these costs expire and flow to the cost of goods sold expense account.

4. Be able to calculate and to understand the significance of the Gross Profit Ratio and the Inventory Turnover Ratio. (p. 150 and pp. 153-154)

The **gross profit ratio** relates the cost of production to the related sales revenue.

It shows how much profit is available to cover selling and administrative costs after the product costs have been deducted. Since there is no absolute value that the gross profit ratio should be, the ratio should be compared within the firm over several years or across companies within the same industry. The gross profit ratio is calculated as follows:

Gross Profit Ratio = Gross Profit/Net Sales

Inventory turnover is a measure of how often during a year the company sells and replaces its inventory. Again, the ratio is meaningful only when it is compared within the firm over several years or across companies within the same industry. The inventory turnover ratio is calculated as follows:

Inventory turnover = Cost of goods sold/Average inventory

5. Understand the significance of the information reported in the income statement. (pp. 154-155)

The primary purpose of the income statement is to provide the user with information about how the entity has performed during the period; that is, how it has used its resources to generate income (or revenues minus expenses).

Even though the amounts reported in the income statement are stated at historical values they can still provide valuable information about the ability of the firm to generate income and cash inflows in the future. The user will examine the operating results of the firm over several periods in order to determine if there are trends in evidence which provide the means to make forecasts about the future.

The separation of income from continuing operations and income from non-continuing operations increases the user's ability to predict the future cash flows.

6. Be able to describe and to illustrate the single–step and the multistep forms of the income statement. (pp. 155-156)

The single–step and multistep forms of the income statement differ primarily in how the revenues and expenses from continuing operations are reported.

The single–step income statement lists all revenues (operational and non–operational) followed by all expenses. The multistep income statement separates operational items from non–operational.

Learning Tip

For an example of single–step and multistep income statements see Exhibits 3-5 and 3-6 on page 157 and 158, respectively, of the text.

7. Know and understand the basic elements of the income statement. (pp. 155-162)

The income statement can contain the following elements: operating items, non–operating items, unusual or infrequent items, income taxes, the results from discontinued operations, and extraordinary items.

Learning Tip

For examples of how each of these elements is presented on the income statement see Exhibits 3-8 and 3-9 on pages 161 and 163 of the text.

Operating income or loss includes revenues and expenses from the normal business activities of a firm; that is, the sale of goods and services. Non–operating income or loss includes revenues and expenses from transactions other than the sale of goods; for example, interest income or expense and gains or losses on the disposal of capital assets. Unusual or infrequent items may be disclosed separately or combined with non–operating items.

Income tax expense, or the provision for income taxes, is the tax expense related to income from continuing operations. Under GAAP, discontinued operations and extraordinary items are disclosed separately and net of related income taxes.

The total income or loss from discontinued operations is reported in two parts: the income or loss from the operation of the segment for the current period up to the date of disposal, and the gain or loss on the disposal of the segment. Both elements are shown net of applicable income taxes.

Extraordinary items have three characteristics: they are **unusual** in the firm's normal business environment, **infrequent** in occurrence, and **not the result of a management decision**. Examples would include a loss on the expropriation of assets in a foreign country or a loss due to an earthquake in Manitoba. Extraordinary items are reported net of applicable income taxes.

Learning Tip

When an extraordinary item results in a gain, the after–tax amount is derived by deducting the applicable income tax from the gain. When an extraordinary item results in a loss, the after–tax amount is derived by deducting the income tax savings from the loss.

Earnings per share (EPS) is reported separately for income from continuing operations, for discontinued operations, and for extraordinary items.

8. Have a firm understanding of the balance sheet elements and its common formats. (pp. 162-167)

The balance sheet may have a **classified** format or an **unclassified** format. In a classified balance sheet current assets and liabilities are separated from noncurrent assets and liabilities.

Current assets are those assets that are either cash or that are capable of being converted into cash within the next twelve months or the normal operating cycle of the company, whichever is longer. Current liabilities are those liabilities that come due within the next twelve months or the normal operating cycle of the company, whichever is longer.

Learning Tip

For examples of these formats see Exhibits 3-11 and 3-12 on pages 165 and 166 of the text.

Some firms present an unclassified balance sheet because they may be a combination of several, very different types of industries.

Assets and liabilities are listed in the order of liquidity. For assets this refers to how quickly the asset can be converted into cash. For liabilities it refers to how quickly the liability will require the use of cash.

9. Be able to identify and account for accrued expenses. (pp. 188-189)

An accrued expense is an expense that has been incurred but has not yet been paid or recorded in the accounts. At the end of an accounting period these items must be identified and recorded. Common examples of accrued expenses are wages, interest, and taxes.

Learning Tip

To record an accrued expense, debit the expense account and credit a related liability account for the amount that has been incurred but not paid. For example, the journal entry to accrue administrative salaries would be as follows:

DR. Salary expense xxx
CR. Salaries payable xxx

Be careful to classify manufacturing costs properly. If the cost is related to production activities, the amount should be debited to Work–In–Process.

Accrued expenses are usually paid in the subsequent accounting period.

Learning Tip

Remember,
Interest expense = principal x interest rate x time

Time is calculated as a fraction of a year.

10. Be able to identify and account for prepaid expenses. (pp.189-191)

A prepaid expense is an amount that has been paid for something that will be received or used in the future. Since, by definition the item has future value and the firm has the right to use it, a prepaid expense is an asset. The cost of a prepaid expense is allocated to the periods in which the item is used up in generating revenue. Examples of prepaid expenses include rent, insurance, and subscription charges. The amortization of a capital asset such as property, plant, and equipment is analogous to the expensing of a prepaid item.

Learning Tip

When payment is made for a service that will be received in the future (such as the prepayment of a three year insurance premium), the amount paid is debited to a Prepaid Expense account. As time passes and the asset is used up (that is, the firm enjoys insurance protection) an appropriate portion of the prepaid amount is debited to an expense account and credited to the prepaid expense account. For example, to recognize the amount of insurance that has been used up on an insurance policy covering the vehicles used by the sales staff: DR. Insurance Expense and CR. Prepaid Insurance.

For assets such as property, plant, and equipment, acquisition costs are debited to noncurrent asset accounts classified as capital assets. The costs are then amortized over the period of time that the asset provides economic benefit to the firm—this period of time is referred to as the useful life of the asset.

For assets used in manufacturing, amortization is charged (debited) to Work-in-Process; otherwise, it is charged to Amortization Expense. In either case, the credit is posted to Accumulated Amortization.

Learning Tip

Accumulated Amortization is a contra-asset account. This means that the account has a credit balance; this, of course, is contrary to normal asset account balances. The accumulated amortization account is increased by credit entries and decreased by debit entries. For reporting purposes, the asset account is shown net of the accumulated amortization amount.

SELF STUDY

MATCHING

Match the key term to the best explanation.

Key Terms

A. Accrued expense
B. Contra–asset
C. Current asset
D. Current liability
E. Prepaid expense
F. Direct costs
G. Extraordinary item
H. Liquidity
I. Overhead costs
J. Earnings per share
K. Finished goods
L. Product costs
M. Raw materials
N. Provision for income taxes
O. Work–in–process

Explanations

1. ___Net income divided by the average number of common shares outstanding during the year.
2. ___Indirect product costs.
3. ___A liability that comes due within the next year.
4. ___An expense that has been incurred but not paid.
5. ___The account that contains the costs of incomplete inventory.
6. ___An item that is unusual, infrequent, and not subject to a decision made by management.
7. ___Accumulated amortization.
8. ___A payment for a service or a product in advance.
9. ___An asset that will be turned into cash within the next year.
10. ___A synonym for income tax expense.
11. ___Consists of direct materials, direct labour, and overhead.
12. ___The inventory account which holds the cost of goods manufactured.
13. ___The ease with which an asset can be converted to cash.
14. ___Production costs that do not include overhead.
15. ___An inventory account whose costs are transferred to the work–in–process account during the production process.

ASSESS YOUR RECALL

1. Discuss the difference between direct and indirect costs and provide two examples of each.

2. Define liquidity as it relates to assets and liabilities.

3. Identify the items on the income statement that are shown net of applicable income taxes.

APPLYING YOUR KNOWLEDGE

1. Classify each of the following costs as either a product cost or a period cost. Then, for the items identified as product costs, further classify them as either a direct cost or an indirect cost.

	Product	Period	Direct	Indirect
a) Plant maintenance	______	______	______	______
b) Product advertising	______	______	______	______
c) Raw materials used	______	______	______	______
d) Production supervisor's salary	______	______	______	______
e) Assembly line wages	______	______	______	______
f) Accounting department operating costs	______	______	______	______
g) Sales staff commissions	______	______	______	______
h) Plant insurance	______	______	______	______
i) Administrative staff salaries	______	______	______	______
j) Plant utilities	______	______	______	______

2. Using the following data, make the calculations required below:

	12/31/X	1/1/X4
Raw materials	5,800	4,500
Work-in-process	20,500	18,700
Finished goods	33,300	38,800
Direct labour	123,000	
Factory utilities	9,600	
Sales commissions	45,000	
Raw materials purchased	66,000	
Factory amortization	75,000	
Insurance (80% manufacturing)	5,500	
Factory maintenance	28,800	
Advertising	80,000	

a. Raw materials used:

b. Cost of goods completed:

c. Cost of goods sold:

3. Prepare the journal entries necessary to record the following transactions that Beasley Manufacturing Ltd. entered into during its second year of operations.

a. Raw material purchases $14,050, of which $3,050 was for cash.

b. Direct labour cost incurred through December 31 was $26,400.

c. Direct labour paid during the year was $27,500.

d. Borrowed $28,000 on April 1 at 9% interest for three years.

e. Sales were $51,600 of which $11,600 was for cash.

f. The beginning balance in taxes payable ($1,250) was paid.

g. Purchased a two-year insurance policy on May 1 for $3,600: (75% of the policy relates to the production facility).

h. Other selling and administrative expenses incurred and paid with cash totalled $1,080.

i. Collected $33,600 from customers on account.

j. Paid suppliers $13,200 on account.

k. Factory wages incurred between December 15 and December 31 were $2,400.

l. Recorded expired insurance for the year.

m. Capital assets with an estimated residual value of $4,000 and an estimated useful life of 8 years totalled $18,000: (80% of these related to production facilities).

n. Accrued interest expense for the year (all administrative).

o. Inventory balances for the year were:

	Beginning	Ending
Raw materials	1,800	1,400
Work-in-process	3,600	5,150
Finished goods	3,000	4,200

p. Income taxes are assessed at 40%, and as of December 31, $1,300 was owed.

	Debit	Credit

	Debit	Credit

4. Bonita, Ltd. is a company located in British Columbia where tornadoes are both unusual and infrequent. During 19X4 the company experienced the following events:

Investment income	1,250
Operating expenses	287,500
Sales	375,000
Earthquake loss	8,750
Operating loss on segment C.	32,500
Gain on disposal of segment C.	50,000
Tax rate	40%
Gain on sale of equipment	3,000
Tornado loss	15,000

a. Prepare a single–step income statement for 19X4.

b. Prepare a multistep income statement for 19X4.

SOLUTIONS TO CHAPTER 3

MATCHING

1.	J	6.	G	11.	L
2.	I	7.	B	12.	K
3.	D	8.	E	13.	H
4.	A	9.	C	14.	F
5.	O	10.	N	15.	M

ASSESS YOUR RECALL

1. Direct production costs are those costs directly and easily traceable to a finished, manufactured product; examples include direct materials and direct labour.

   Indirect production costs are all other costs incurred in the production process. These costs, also known as overhead costs, would include any other production costs such as factory supplies, factory amortization, production supervision salaries, and factory insurance.

2. For assets, liquidity refers to how quickly the asset can be converted to cash. For liabilities, liquidity refers to how quickly the liability will require the use of cash; that is, its maturity date.

3. Discontinued operations:
   Income/loss on operations up to date of disposal
   Gain/loss on disposal of segment
   Extraordinary items

APPLYING YOUR KNOWLEDGE

1.

	Product	Period	Direct	Indirect
a. Plant maintenance	X			X
b. Product advertising		X		
c. Raw materials used	X		X	
d. Production supervisor's salary	X			X
e. Assembly line wages	X		X	
f. Accounting department operating costs		X		
g. Sales staff commissions		X		
h. Plant insurance	X			X
i. Administrative staff salaries		X		
j. Plant utilities	X			X

2\. a.

Beginning balance	$ 4,500
Purchases	66,000
Total available	70,500
Less: Ending balance	5,800
Raw materials used	$ 64,700

b.

Beginning balance	$ 18,700
Direct labour	123,000
Raw materials used	64,700
Factory utilities	9,600
Factory amortization	75,000
Insurance (5,500 x 80%)	4,400
Factory maintenance	28,800
Total	324,200
Less: Ending balance	20,500
Cost of goods completed	$303,700

c.

Beginning balance	$ 38,800
Cost of goods completed	303,700
Total	342,500
Less: Ending balance	33,300
Cost of goods sold	$309,200

3\.

	Debit	Credit
a. Raw Materials	14,050	
Accounts Payable		11,000
Cash		3,050
b. Work-in-Process	26,400	
Salaries & Wages Payable		26,400
c. Salaries & Wages Payable	27,500	
Cash		27,500
d. Cash	28,000	
Notes Payable (long-term)		28,000
e. Cash	11,600	
Accounts Receivable	40,000	
Sales		51,600

f.	Taxes Payable	1,250	
	Cash		1,250
g.	Prepaid Insurance	3,600	
	Cash		3,600
h.	Other Selling & Administrative Exp.	1,080	
	Cash		1,080
i.	Cash	33,600	
	Accounts Receivable		33,600
j.	Accounts Payable	13,200	
	Cash		13,200
k.	Work-in-Process	2,400	
	Salaries & Wages Payable		2,400
l.	Work-in-Process [(3,600/2)x(2/3)x75%]	900	
	Insurance Expense [(3,600/2)x(2/3)x25%]	300	
	Prepaid Insurance		1,200
m.	Work-in-Process [(18,000−4,000)/8]x80%	1,400	
	Amortization Expense (1,750−1,400)	350	
	Accumulated Amortization		1,750
n.	Interest Expense (28,000x.09x.75)	1,890	
	Interest Payable		1,890
o.	Work-in-Process (1,800+14,050−1,400)	14,450	
	Raw Materials		14,450
	Finished Goods*	44,000	
	Work-in-Process		44,000
	*(3,600+26,400+2,400+900+1,400+14,450−5,150)		
	Cost of Goods Sold (3,000+44,000−4,200)	42,800	
	Finished Goods		42,800
p.	Income Tax Expense*	2,072	
	Income Taxes Payable		2,072
	*(51,600−42,800−300−350−1,080−1,890)x.40		

4. a.

Bonita, Ltd.
Income Statement
For the Year Ended December 31, 19X4

Revenues:		
Sales	$375,000	
Investment income	1,250	
Gain on sale of equipment	3,000	
Total revenues		$379,250
Expenses:		
Operating expenses	287,500	
Earthquake loss	8,750	
Total expenses		296,250
Income before taxes		83,000
Provision for taxes		33,200
Income from continuing operations		49,800
Discontinued operations:		
Operating loss (net of $13,000 tax savings)	(19,500)	
Gain on disposal (net of $20,000 taxes)	30,000	10,500
Income before extraordinary item		60,300
Loss from tornado (net of $6,000 tax savings)		(9,000)
Net Income		$51,300

b.

Bonita, Ltd.
Income Statement
For the Year Ended December 31, 19X4

Sales	$375,000	
Operating expenses	287,500	
Income from operations		$87,500
Other income/expense:		
Investment income	1,250	
Gain on sale of equipment	3,000	
Earthquake loss	(8,750)	(4,500)
Income before taxes		83,000
Provision for taxes		33,200
Income continuing operations		49,800
Discontinued operations:		
Operating loss (net of $13,000 tax savings)	(19,500)	
Gain on disposal (net of $20,000 taxes)	30,000	10,500
Income before extraordinary item		60,300
Loss from tornado (net of $6,000 tax savings)		(9,000)
Net Income		51,300

CHAPTER 4

REVENUE RECOGNITION

CHAPTER OVERVIEW

This chapter continues the discussion begun in Chapter 2 on revenue recognition and performance measurement. It is pointed out that what is really being measured is the change in owners' wealth. One common measure of performance is the **return on investment** (ROI); another measure is the change in value of the shareholders' equity accounts. The need to measure change in value leads to the need for concepts and guidelines for revenue recognition. These guidelines help to ensure that the changes in value are measured on a consistent basis and on a conceptually sound basis.

The cash-to-cash cycle is introduced as a model for determining when revenue should be recognized. This cycle outlines the steps involved in converting cash into inventory, selling the inventory, and then converting the receivables back into cash. Performance can be measured at various points within this cycle.

The revenue recognition criteria introduced in Chapter 2 are now developed further. The criteria consist of two general concepts: the revenue must be measureable and it must have probable future benefit. In addition, the revenue must be earned and must be realized or realizable. If all of these conditions are met, the revenue should be recognized.

Revenue recognition at different points within the cash-to-cash cycle include the following: at the time of sale; at the time of contract signing; at the time of production; and at the time of collection.

LEARNING OBJECTIVES

1. Be familiar with the elements of the cash-to-cash cycle.
2. Understand the revenue recognition criteria.
3. Be familiar with the criteria for revenue recognition at the time of sale or shipment to the customer.
4. Be familiar with the criteria for revenue recognition at the time of contract signing.
5. Be able to apply the completed contract method and the percentage of completion method of revenue recognition.
6. Be able to apply the instalment method and the cost recovery method of revenue recognition.
7. Understand Return on Investment and net income as measures of performance.

CHAPTER REVIEW

1. Be familiar with the elements of the cash-to-cash cycle. (pp. 215–218)

The cash-to-cash cycle is a model that describes the process of converting cash into inventory, selling the inventory, and converting the subsequent receivables back into cash. The steps for a manufacturing firm include the following: the initial investment of cash; the purchase of raw materials; production; selling activity; delivery of the product (including any warranty service); and the ultimate collection of the receivable.

Learning Tip

For a graphic representation of this model see Exhibit 4-1 on page 216 of the text.

The terms of a sale may include a cash discount offer to encourage prompt payment of the receivable. A typical discount might be 2/10, net 30. This means that the purchaser will receive a 2% discount if payment is made within 10 days of the invoice date; otherwise, the entire amount is due within 30 days.

2. Understand the revenue recognition criteria. (pp. 218–221)

Before revenue may be recognized and reported in the financial statements it must meet two general criteria: it must be measureable—that is, there must be a reasonable basis for estimating the amount; and it must have probable future benefit to the firm. Two additional, more specific, criteria require that the revenue has been earned—that is, the earnings process is substantially complete; and that revenues are realized or realizeable.

Learning Tip

For an explanation of the revenue recognition criteria see pp. 219–221 of the text.

A revenue is **earned** when a firm has substantially completed what it must do to be entitled to receive the associated benefits from the sale.

A revenue is **realized** when cash or other assets are received at the date of the sale. A revenue is **realizable** if the noncash assets received are readily convertible to a known amount of cash.

3. Be familiar with the criteria for revenue recognition at the time of sale or shipment to the customer. (pp. 222–223)

The most common revenue recognition point is at the time the title to the goods passes to the customer or services are completed in conformity with a contract.

Goods may be sold F.O.B. shipping point or F.O.B. destination. These two designations indicate both when title to the goods passes from seller to buyer and which party bears the risks of ownership; that is, who must pay for freight, insurance, and other charges.

Learning Tip

F.O.B. shipping point means that title to the goods passes to the buyer when the goods leave the seller's place of business. The buyer is responsible for freight or other charges. F.O.B. destination means that title passes to the buyer when the goods reach the buyer's place of business. In this case, the seller is responsible for freight and other charges.

If cash is received in advance of shipping the goods or providing the services, the transaction should be recorded as a liability not a revenue. Until the seller has provided the goods or services a liability exists. The seller must either provide the goods or services or return the cash.

Learning Tip

Cash received in advance is recognized as a deferred revenue and recorded in a liability account with the title of "revenue received in advance" or "deposits from customers".

4. Be familiar with the criteria for revenue recognition at the time of contract signing. (pp. 223–224)

The two primary examples of revenue recognized at the time of contract signing are the sale of franchises and the sale of retail land. The two criteria that must be met are that substantially all of the costs associated with the sale have been incurred, and that any receivable created by the sale is reasonably collectible.

5. Be able to apply the completed contract method and the percentage of completion method of revenue recognition. (pp. 224–226)

The timing of revenue recognition on long-term construction projects is one example of recognizing revenue at the time of production. Another example is certain mining operations where the market value and the sale of the production are both reasonably assured at the time of production.

Under the completed contract method the recognition of revenues and expenses is deferred until the project is completed. Therefore, profit is reported only in the year of completion.

Under the percentage of completion method a portion of project revenue and expenses is recognized in each year of the construction project based on the percentage that the contract is complete. One method of estimating the percentage of completion is by calculating the ratio of costs incurred to total estimated costs.

Learning Tip

The percentage of completion is determined as follows:

$$\frac{\text{costs incurred for the current period}}{\text{estimated total costs on the project}}$$

The revenue recognized each year is equal to the percentage of completion multiplied by the contract price. For an example, see Exhibit 4-3 on page 226 of the text.

Under either method, if an overall loss is projected on the project, the loss must be recognized as soon as it can be estimated.

6. Be able to apply the instalment method and the cost recovery method of revenue recognition. (pp. 227–228)

The instalment method is appropriate when the collectability of the related receivable is not reasonably assured. Under this method the buyer agrees to make periodic payments usually over a long period of time. Each payment is viewed as consisting of three elements: cost recovery, profit, and interest.

Learning Tip

Compute the gross profit percentage on each sale as follows:

$$\text{Gross profit \%} = \frac{\text{Sales price} - \text{Cost}}{\text{Sales price}}$$

Determine the portion of each payment to be applied against the principal as follows:

$$\text{Principal portion} = \text{Cash received} - \text{Interest}$$

Calculate the amount of gross profit to recognize as follows:

$$\text{Gross profit} = \text{Principal portion} \times \text{Gross profit \%}$$

For an example, see Exhibit 4-4 on page 228 of the text.

The cost recovery method is appropriate when collection of the related receivable is in serious doubt. Under this method, profit recognition is deferred until the cost of the item sold has been recovered. Recognition of interest can occur with cost recovery or be postponed until after cost recovery occurs.

Learning Tip

Determine the amount of cost recovery in each payment as follows:

$$\text{Cost recovery} = \text{Payment received} - \text{Interest}$$

After the cost of the item sold has been recovered, gross profit is determined as follows:

$$\text{Gross profit} = \text{Payment received} - \text{Interest}$$

For an example, see Exhibit 4-5 on page 228 of the text.

7. Understand the Return on Investment and net income as measures of performance. (pp. 213–215)

Return on investment (ROI) is a ratio which the shareholders of a company will use to calculate how well their investment in the firm is performing. The ratio is calculated as follows:

$$\text{ROI} = \frac{\text{Return}}{\text{Average investment}}$$

The numerator can be, for example, interest earned on the investment or the net income of the company. The denominator is the average amount that has been committed to the investment during a period of time (usually one year). To determine if the performance of the investment is adequate, the ROI will be compared to other potential investments that the users might have chosen.

SELF STUDY

MATCHING

Match the key term to the best explanation.

Key Terms

A. Cash discount
B. Cash-to-cash cycle
C. Completed contract
D. Cost recovery
E. Earned
F. F.O.B. Destination
G. F.O.B. Shipping Point
H. Installment
I. Matching principle
J. Percentage of completion
K. Realizeable
L. Realized
M. Return on Investment

Explanation

1. ___ When cash or noncash assets are received on the date of a sale.
2. ___ Indicates that title to the goods passes to the buyer when the goods leave the seller's place of business.
3. ___ A method that defers recognition of any profit until the cash collected equals the cost of the item sold.
4. ___ A reduction in the amount owed if payment is received within a specified time period.
5. ___ Requires that expenses be recognized in the same period as the revenues that they generated.
6. ___ Indicates that the earnings process is substantially complete.
7. ___ Net income divided by average investment.
8. ___ Recognizes revenue each year in proportion to the costs incurred that year relative to total estimated costs.
9. ___ When the noncash assets received from a sale are readily convertible into a known amount of cash.
10. ___ Indicates that title to the goods passes to the buyer when the goods arrive at the buyer's place of business.
11. ___ Describes the activities a firm engages in from the initial investment of cash to the production of inventory and the subsequent collection of cash from the sale of inventory.
12. ___ Defers recognition of revenue until a project is finished.
13. ___ A method in which each payment is viewed as consisting of cost recovery, profit, and interest.

ASSESS YOUR RECALL

1. Outline the steps, in the proper order, of the cash-to-cash cycle for a grocery store.

2. Identify the conditions that must be met in order for revenue to be recognized.

3. Indicate when income is first recognized under:

   a. percentage of completion method;
   b. instalment method;
   c. completed contract method;
   d. cost recovery method.

APPLYING YOUR KNOWLEDGE

1. During 19X1, Dominion Construction Ltd. agreed to build an office building for a price of $750,000. Costs incurred over the life of the project were: 19X1—$225,000; 19X2—$255,000; 19X3—$120,000. Determine the revenue, expense, and profit/loss for each year using:

   a. the completed contract method;

   b. the percentage of completion method.

2. Superior Construction Ltd. signed a contract in 19X1 to construct a building for $800,000. Costs were originally estimated to be: 19X1—$208,000; 19X2—$156,000; 19X3—$104,000; 19X4—$52,000. The costs for 19X1 and 19X2 were incurred as estimated. Before the books were closed for 19X2, the estimated costs for the remaining two years of the project were revised to: 19X3—$254,000; and 19X4—$192,000. The company uses the percentage of completion method. Determine the revenue, expense, and profit/loss for each year.

3. Chesley Furniture Ltd. sold $200,000 (cost $160,000) of office furniture to a customer in 19X1 with the following payment plan: 19X1—$40,000; 19X2—$50,000; 19X3—$75,000; 19X4—$90,000. Interest is to be spread evenly over the four years. Compute the revenue, expense, gross profit, and interest income for each year, using:

a. the instalment method method;

b. the cost recovery method.

SOLUTIONS TO CHAPTER 4

MATCHING

1.	L	6.	E	10.	F
2.	G	7.	M	11.	B
3.	D	8.	J	12.	C
4.	A	9.	K	13.	H
5.	I				

ASSESS YOUR RECALL

1. Cash→ purchase inventory→ selling activities→ delivery of product and collection → cash

2. Revenue must be measureable, it must have probable future benefit, the earnings process must be substantially complete, and the revenue must be realized or realizeable.

3. a. When progress is made on a contract as evidenced by the incurrence of construction costs.

   b. When the first cash payment is received.

   c. When the contract has been completed.

   d. When the cost of the item sold has been recovered.

APPLYING YOUR KNOWLEDGE

1.

a.

	19X1	19X2	19X3
Revenue	$ 0	$ 0	$750,000
Expenses	0	0	600,000
Profit	$ 0	$ 0	$150,000

b.

	19X1	19X2	19X3
Revenue	$281,250*	$318,750	$150,000
Expenses	225,000	255,000	120,000
Profit	$ 56,250	$ 63,750	$ 30,000

*(225,000/600,000)/750,000

2.

	19X1	19X2*	19X3	19X3
Revenue	$320,000	$——	$254,000	$192,000
Expenses	208,000	——	254,000	192,000
Profit(loss)	$112,000	$(122,000)	$ 0	$ 0

*19X1 and 19X2 costs	$364,000
19X3 and 19X4 estimated costs	446,000
Total estimated costs to complete	810,000
Less: contract price	800,000
Estimated contract loss	10,000
Plus: 19X1 profit	112,000
19X2 loss	$122,000

**Assuming the new estimated costs remain unchanged, there will be no additional profits or losses, and revenues will equal expenses.

3.

a.	19X1	19X2	19X3	19X4
Revenue	$26,250	$36,250	$61,250	$76,250
Expenses	21,000	29,000	49,000	61,000
Gross Profit	$ 5,250	$ 7,250	$12,250	$15,250
Interest Income	$13,750	$13,750	$13,750	$13,750

Interest = (total payments − sales price)/4
Revenue = payment − interest
GP% = (sales price − cost)/sales price = 20%
Gross profit = revenue x GP%
Expenses = revenue − gross profit

b.	19X1	19X2	19X3	19X4
Revenue	$26,250	$36,250	$61,250	$76,250
Expenses	26,250	36,250	61,250	36,250
Gross Profit	$ 0	$ 0	$ 0	$40,000
Interest Income	$13,750	$13,750	$13,750	$13,750

CHAPTER 5

MANAGEMENT OF CASH AND STATEMENT OF CHANGES IN FINANCIAL POSITION

CHAPTER OVERVIEW

In chapter four performance was measured in terms of net income. In this chapter performance is measured by examining a firm's cash generating ability.

The chapter begins by providing an example of cash flow problems often encountered by start-up companies: under-capitalization, rapid growth, and significant lead/lag relationships in cash (inflows and outflows). It then illustrates some possible solutions to these problems.

The statement of changes in financial position (SCFP), or statement of cash flows, is then discussed in terms of its history, components, format, and disclosures. The components of the statement are the cash flows from operating activities, investing activities, and financing activities (the same activities introduced in Chapter One). The cash flows from operating activities may be presented using either the direct approach or the indirect approach.

Preparation of the SCFP requires an analysis of the income statement, balance sheet, and other financial data. The chapter demonstrates how to use T-accounts to perform this analysis. The result is a cash T-account that contains all of the elements necessary to prepare the SCFP.

Last, the chapter presents some insights into how to analyze the information contained in the SCFP. Users are often interested in using current data to predict future cash flows. This can be done by separating continuing cash flows from non-continuing cash flows. Then the user must determine if the cash flows from operating activities are sufficient to cover the investing and financing activities in the long run. One way to make this determination is to review the operating cash flows of the company over the previous five years.

LEARNING OBJECTIVES

1. Be aware of the cash flow problems typically encountered by start-up and rapid growth firms.
2. Be familiar with the components of the statement of changes in financial position.
3. Understand how to format the statement of changes in financial position.
4. Be able to construct a statement of changes in financial position using the T-account approach.
5. Be able to interpret the information contained in the statement of changes in financial position.

CHAPTER REVIEW

1. Be aware of the cash flow problems typicallyencountered by start-up and rapid growth firms. (pp. 251–259)

Rapid growth and start-up companies typically encounter three problems that adversely affect their cash flows: high growth rates in sales, under-capitalization, and significant lead/lag relationships in cash inflows and outflows.

A high growth rate requires a firm to increase production and expand capacity—both of which require additional cash. A possible solution is to slow the growth rate but this action may cause potential customers to take their business to competitors.

Under-capitalization is caused by starting the firm with insufficient cash. Possible solutions to this problem include borrowing cash or issuing additional shares to investors. Unfortunately, each of these solutions has potential negative ramifications. Borrowed cash must be repaid with interest and additional issued capital will result in the payment of increased amounts of dividends and could result in some loss of control.

Lead/lag relationships are based on the timing of the cash outflows for production costs and the cash inflows from sales. There is usually a time lag between the production and sale of goods and another time lag between the sale of goods on account and the collection of cash. A firm could try to change its accounts receivable, accounts payable, and/or inventory policies to improve the lead/lag relationship. Alternatively, the firm could consider either raising the selling price of its goods or reducing the costs of production. All of these alternatives have potentially negative consequences; for example, increasing selling price or decreasing discounts offered to customers or reducing inventory on hand may result in lost sales.

2. Be familiar with the components of the statement of changes in financial position. (pp. 260–263)

The major components of the SCFP are the cash flows resulting from a firm's operating, investing, and financing activities. For the purposes of the SCFP cash is defined as **cash and cash equivalents**. Cash equivalents include short-term, highly liquid investments, that are convertible into known amounts of cash. Cash equivalents are shown net of short-term borrowings.

Learning Tip

Examples of cash equivalents include Government of Canada Treasury Bills, certificates of deposit, and demand loans of other corporations.

Cash equivalents = Cash + Short-term investments – short-term borrowings

Cash flows from operating activities include those resulting from the sale of goods and services to customers, collections on those sales, payments for acquisition or production of inventory, and payments for cash operating expenses (including interest and taxes).

Cash flows from investing activities are the result of acquiring and/or selling noncurrent assets such as investments in long-term marketable securities or property, plant, and equipment.

Cash flows from financing activities are the result from incurring and repaying debt, from issuing and repurchasing the firm's share capital and from paying dividends.

Learning Tip

Interest payments on debt and interest or dividends received on investments are considered operating cash flows.

3. Understand how to format the SCFP. (p. 263)

Two approaches are allowed for the SCFP: the direct approach and the indirect approach. The difference between these approaches is limited to the operating activities section of the statements. Both approaches use the same format to present investing and financing cash flows.

The **direct** approach presents the gross cash flows from each operating activity; for example, collections from customers and payments to suppliers.

The **indirect** approach derives net cash flow from operations by adjusting net income for the noncash income statement items and for changes in the working capital accounts.

Learning Tip

For an example of the indirect approach see Exhibit 5-11 on page 261 of the text.

4. Be able to construct a statement of changes in financial position using the T-account approach. (pp. 264–271)

Preparation of the SCFP requires an analysis of the data found in the income statement, the balance sheet, and the company records. To accomplish this analysis in an orderly manner a T-account may be used. The result will be a cash T-account that contains all of the data necessary to prepare the operating, investing, and financing activities sections of the statement.

Learning Tip

For an example of how to apply the T-account approach see page 266 for the indirect method and see Exhibit 5A-26 on page 309 for the direct method.

Under the direct method start with the transactions that are most easily identifiable; that is, those that appear in the income statement.

Learning Tip

Outlined below are several equations that can be used to determine, or verify, the cash flow amounts for certain operating activities.

Collections from customers = Sales ± Change in A/R
(+ for decrease, – for increase)

Inventory purchases = Cost of goods sold ± Change in Inventory
(+ for increase – for decrease)

Payments to suppliers = Purchases ± Change in A/P
(+ for decrease – for increase)

Payments for any cash expense = Expense ± Change in related payable
(+ for decrease – for increase)

Payments for prepaid expense = Expense ± Change in related prepaid expense
(+ for increase. – for decrease)

Payments for dividends = Dividends declared ± Change in dividends pay
(+ for decrease – for increase)

The debits in the cash T-account represent sources of cash and the credits, uses of cash.

Under the indirect approach the analysis should be performed in the following order to ensure that all cash flows are recognized: net income, noncash items on the income statement, and changes in the working capital accounts.

Learning Tip

Under this approach net income is initially viewed as an increase to cash. However, because net income contains certain noncash items it must be adjusted for those items. Outlined below are the adjustments to net income and the increases/decreases in cash using the indirect approach.

Adjustments to net income:

Increase net income for amortization or for a loss on the sale of property, plant, and equipment or investments.

Decrease net income for a gain on sale of property, plant, and equipment or investments.

Increases to cash:

Decrease in any current asset
Increase in any current liability

Decreases to cash:

Increase in any current asset
Decrease in any current liability

The debits to the cash T-account represent either an adjustment to net income or an increase to cash, while the credits represent either an adjustment to net income or a use of cash.

5. Be able to interpret the information contained in the statement of changes in financial position. (pp. 272–276)

Users of the SCFP are interested in the firm's cash generating performance during the current period but are more interested in predicting future cash flows. Cash flow prediction is facilitated by separating continuing cash flows from noncontinuing cash flows. The user can then determine whether continuing cash flows from operating activities will be sufficient to cover future cash flows from the other two activities. This process is facilitated by reviewing the continuing cash flows for the firm over the previous five years.

Continuing sources of cash include operating activities (that is, the sale of a firm's goods and services), the acquisition of debt, and the issuance of share capital. Continuing uses of cash include the purchase of property, plant, and equipment, the payment of loan principal and interest, and the payment of dividends.

Learning Tip

The analysis of cash from operations is best performed using the indirect approach because this approach highlights how a firm is managing its receivables, inventory, and payables.

If a firm is expanding, accounts receivable, inventory, and accounts payable should all increase. If this relationship is not indicated on the SCFP then the user should attempt to discover the reason for the discrepancy.

SELF STUDY

MATCHING

Match the key term to the best explanation.

Key Terms

A. Capitalization
B. Cash equivalents
C. Direct approach
D. Financing activities
E. Indirect approach
F. Investing activities
G. Lead/lag relationship
H. Operating activities

Explanation

1. C Derives cash from operations based on gross cash receipts and payments.
2. F Includes outflows for the purchase of equipment.
3. A The dollar amount of the resources contributed by owners and debtholders.
4. E Derives cash from operations by adjusting net income for noncash expenses and revenues.
5. B Cash plus short-term, highly liquid investments that are readily convertible into known amounts of cash minus short-term borrowings.
6. H Includes cash flows from the sale of goods and services to customers.
7. D Includes the payment of cash dividends.
8. G The timing difference between cash outflows for expenses and cash inflows from revenues.

ASSESS YOUR RECALL

1. Explain why net income is not equivalent to the increase in cash and provide two examples for the difference.

2. Define the term **cash equivalents** and provide two examples.

3. The direct and indirect approaches derive cash flows from operations differently. List three examples of line items that would appear under each approach.

4. Indicate the section of the statement of changes in financial position (operating, investing, or financing) in which each of the following would appear.

Item	Section
Interest payments	O - Ind.
Dividend payments	F
Loss on sale of marketable securities	O - Ind
Change in accounts payable	O - "
Interest income received	O - dir
Income tax payments	O - dir
Dividends received	O - dir
Repurchase of own shares	F
Proceeds from sale of equipment	I
Net loss	O - indirect

APPLYING YOUR KNOWLEDGE

Given the following information:

Medicine Hat Sales Ltd.
Income Statement
For the Year Ended December 31, 19X5

Sales		$333,900
Expenses:		
Cost of goods sold	$157,500	
Salaries expense	86,400	
Interest expense	14,400	
Insurance expense	1,100	
Amortization expense	25,000	
Loss on sale of equipment	9,000	
Income taxes expense	16,200	
Total expenses		309,600
Net income		$ 24,300

Additional information:
(1) Equipment originally costing $63,000 was sold for $46,100.
(2) A building was purchased for $73,800.
(3) Dividends of $18,000 were declared and paid.

Medicine Hat Sales Ltd.
Comparative Balance Sheets

	19X5	19X4
Assets		
Cash	$ 19,920	$ 45,900
Accounts receivable	60,000	105,000
Inventory	90,000	54,000
Prepaid insurance	3,000	1,200
Total current assets	172,920	206,100
Property, plant & equipment	307,800	297,000
Accumulated amortization	(128,520)	(111,420)
Total noncurrent assets	179,280	185,580
Total assets	$ 352,200	$ 391,680
Liabilities & Shareholders' Equity		
Accounts payable	$ 51,300	$ 69,480
Salaries payable	21,600	43,200
Income taxes payable	2,000	10,000

Total current liabilities	74,900	122,680
Notes payable	70,000	80,000
Total liabilities	144,900	202,680
Common shares	192,000	180,000
Retained earnings	15,300	9,000
Total liabilities & equity	$352,200	$391,680

1. Prepare a statement of changes in financial position for 19X5 supported by T-accounts. Use the direct approach for the operating activities section.

2. Prepare the operating activities section of the statement of changes in financial position using the indirect approach supported by T-accounts.

SOLUTIONS TO CHAPTER 5

MATCHING

1. C	5. B
2. F	6. H
3. A	7. D
4. E	8. G

ASSESS YOUR RECALL

1. Net income measures performance at a particular point in the cash-to-cash cycle and, therefore, it ignores all the lead/lag relationships in cash flows. For example, net income reflects revenues earned but not necessarily the cash collected from customers. Net income also reflects expenses incurred but not necessarily the cash paid to suppliers or employees.

2. Cash equivalents are short-term, highly liquid investments that are convertible into known amounts of cash. Cash equivalents are also net of short-term borrowings. Examples include Government of Canada Treasury bills and certificates of deposit.

3. Direct:
    - Collections from customers
    - Interest or dividends received
    - Payments to suppliers
    - Payments to employees
    - Payments for interest and/or income taxes

   Indirect:
    - Net income or loss
    - Adjustments for amortization and gains or losses on sale of PP&E or investments
    - Changes in working capital accounts

4.

Item	Section
Interest payments	Operating-direct
Dividend payments	Financing
Loss on sale of marketable securities	Operating-indirect
Change in accounts payable	Operating-indirect
Interest income received	Operating-direct
Income tax payments	Operating-direct
Dividends received	Operating-direct
Repurchase of own shares	Financing
Proceeds from sale of equipment	Investing
Net loss	Operating-indirect

APPLYING YOUR KNOWLEDGE

1. Direct approach

A-Cash

	(✓)	45,900			
Operating:					
Coll. from cust.	(2)	378,900	211,680	(5)	Pmts. to suppliers
			108,000	(7)	Pmts. to employees
			14,400	(8)	Pmts. for interest
			2,900	(10)	Pmts. for insurance
Investing:			24,200	(12)	Pmts. for taxes
Proceeds from sale of equip.	(15)	46,100	73,800	(14)	Purch. of bldg
Financing:					
Issue of shares	(17)	12,000	10,000	(16)	Pmt. on note pay
			18,000	(18)	Pmt. of dividend
	(✓)	19,920			

A-Accts Receivable

(✓)	105,000		
(1)	333,900	378,900	(2)
(✓)	60,000		

L-Accts Payable

		69,480	(✓)
(5)	211,680	193,500	(4)
		51,300	(✓)

A-Inventory

(✓)	54,000		
(4)	193,500	157,500	(3)
(✓)	90,000		

L-Salaries Payable

		43,200	(✓)
(7)	108,000	86,400	(6)
		21,600	(✓)

A-Prepaid Insurance

(✓)	1,200		
(10)	2,900	1,100	(9)
(✓)	3,000		

L-Taxes Payable

		10,000	(✓)
(12)	24,200	16,200	(11)
		2,000	(✓)

A-PP&E

(✓)	297,000		
(13)	73,800	63,000	(15)
(✓)	307,800		

L-Notes Payable

		80,000	(✓)
(16)	10,000		
		70,000	(✓)

XA-Accum. Amortization

		111,420	(✓)
(15)	7,900	25,000	(14)
		128,520	(✓)

SE-Common Shares

		180,000	(✓)
		12,000	(17)
		192,000	(✓)

Retained Earnings

(3)	157,500	9,000	(✓)
(6)	86,400	333,900	(1)
(8)	14,400		
(9)	1,100		
(11)	16,200		
(13)	25,000		
(15)	9,000		
(18)	18,000		
		15,300	(✓)

Medicine Hat Sales Ltd.
Statement of Changes in Financial Position
For the Year Ended December 31, 19X5

Operating activities:		
Collections from customers	$378,900	
Payments to suppliers	(211,680)	
Payments to employees	(108,000)	
Payments for interest	(14,400)	
Payments for insurance	(2,900)	
Payments for income taxes	(24,200)	
Cash provided by operating activities		$17,720
Investing activities:		
Proceeds from sale of equipment	46,100	
Purchase of building	(73,800)	
Cash used by investing activities		(27,700)
Financing activities:		
Issuance of common shares	12,000	
Payment on note payable	(10,000)	
Payment of dividends	(18,000)	
Cash used by financing activities		(16,000)
Net decrease in cash		(25,980)
Cash balance, December 31, 19X4		45,900
Cash balance, December 31, 19X5		$19,920

2. Indirect approach

A-Cash

		Debit	Credit		
	(✓)	45,900			
Operating:					
Net income	(1)	24,300	36,000	(5)	Inventory increase
Amortization	(2)	25,000	1,800	(6)	Prepd. ins. incr.
Loss on sale			18,180	(7)	A/P decrease
of equipment	(3)	9,000	21,600	(8)	Salaries pay. decr.
A/R increase	(4)	45,000	8,000	(9)	Tax pay. decr.
Investing:					
Proceeds from sale					
of equipment	(3)	46,100			

A-Accts Receivable

	Debit	Credit	
(✓)	105,000		
(1)		45,000	(4)
(✓)	60,000		

L-Accts Payable

	Debit	Credit	
		69,480	(✓)
(7)	18,180		
		51,300	(✓)

A-Inventory

	Debit	Credit	
(✓)	54,000		
(4)	36,000		
(✓)	90,000		

L-Salaries Payable

	Debit	Credit	
		43,200	(✓)
(8)	21,600		
		21,600	(✓)

A-Prepaid Insurance

	Debit	Credit	
(✓)	1,200		
(6)	1,800		
(✓)	3,000		

L-Taxes Payable

	Debit	Credit	
		10,000	(✓)
(12)	8,000		
		2,000	(✓)

A-PP&E

	Debit	Credit	
(✓)	297,000		
	63,000		(3)

SE-Retained Earnings

	Debit	Credit	
		9,000	(✓)
		24,300	(1)

XA-Accum. Amortization

	Debit	Credit	
		111,420	(✓)
(3)	7,900	25,000	(2)
		128,520	(✓)

Operating Activities:		
Net income	$24,300	
Adjustments to reconcile net income to cash provided from operations:		
Amortization	25,000	
Loss on sale of equipment	9,000	
Changes in working capital:		
Decrease in accts. receivable	45,000	
Increase in inventory	(36,000)	
Increase in Prepd. insurance	(1,800)	
Decrease in accounts payable	(18,180)	
Decrease in salaries payable	(21,600)	
Decrease in taxes payable	(8,000)	
Cash provided by operating activities		$17,720

Note: The investing and financing activities would be derived in the same manner as the direct approach in (1) above.

CHAPTER 6

CASH, TEMPORARY INVESTMENTS, AND ACCOUNTS RECEIVABLE

CHAPTER OVERVIEW

This chapter discusses the recognition, valuation, recording, reporting, and statement analysis considerations of cash, accounts receivable, and temporary investments.

Cash meets both asset recognition criteria. It is valued at its face value as required by the unit of measure assumption. Possession of a foreign currency on the date of the balance sheet requires a conversion into Canadian dollars.

Temporary investments meet the asset recognition criteria when a firm holds shares or treasury bills and owns the right to future dividend or interest payments and the right to future sales prices. Equity securities are valued using the lower of cost and market method. Unrealized losses and recoveries of unrealized losses on the current portfolio of equity securities are recognized on the income statement.

Asset recognition for accounts receivable is met by evidence of a formal or informal contractual agreement and by the right to receive future payments on the accounts. Accounts receivable are valued at their gross amount less allowances for uncollectible accounts, returns, and discounts. Bad debt expense can be recognized using either the direct write-off method which violates the matching principle or by the allowance method. The allowance method can be applied by using the percentage of credit sales method or the ageing of accounts receivable method.

LEARNING OBJECTIVES

1. Understand the conceptual basis for the recognition and valuation of cash.
2. Understand how the current portfolio of temporary investments is recognized, valued, recorded, and reported.
3. Understand how accounts receivable are recognized, valued, recorded, and reported.
4. Be familiar with the recognition, valuation, recording, and reporting of notes receivable.
5. Be aware of how cash, accounts receivable, and temporary investments contribute to financial statement analysis.

CHAPTER REVIEW

1. Understand the conceptual basis for the recognition and valuation of cash. (pp. 315–316)

Cash meets the ownership, or right to use, criterion for asset recognition. It also meets the probable future value criterion even though there may be some uncertainty about its future purchasing power.

Under GAAP, according to the unit of measure assumption, cash is valued at its face value. Foreign currency held at the date of the financial statements must be converted to Canadian dollars. Conversion is calculated by using the exchange rate on the date of the balance sheet. Any gain or loss on the translation to Canadian dollars is recognized on the income statement as a **foreign currency transaction gain/loss**.

Since cash is the most liquid asset and since it is the medium of exchange, it is susceptible to theft and must be carefully safeguarded. Management safeguards assets by instituting controls over the assets; that is, controls are procedures designed, in part, to prevent or detect fraudulent activity. Cash can be safeguarded by ensuring that functions related to cash—signing authority, recording of transactions, authorization of payments, and reconciliation of the asset to the records—are carried out by different persons. The bank reconciliation is a particulary effective control over cash provided that it is performed on a regular basis and by someone with no conflicting duties. A bank reconciliation is a procedure which brings into agreement (that is, reconciles) the cash balance per the accounting records to the cash balance per the bank. Some differences in the two records which have to be taken into account are the following: items recorded on the books but not yet recorded by the bank—for example, outstanding cheques or deposits; items recorded by the bank but not yet recorded in the books—for example, service charges or interest; and errors in the accounting records or the bank records.

Learning Tip

For an example of a foreign currency conversion into Canadian dollars see Exhibit 6-1 on page 317 of the text.

2. Understand how the current portfolio of temporary investments is recognized, valued, recorded, and reported (pp. 320–327)

Marketable equity securities included in the portfolio of temporary investments consist of investments in the shares of other companies. These are classified as current if management's intention is to hold the securities for less than one year and if there is no intention of acquiring the shares in order to exercise control over the other company.

The ownership, or right to use, criterion is evidenced either by a share certificate or by an open account with a broker. The probable future value criterion is met by the right to receive any declared dividends and by the right to sell the share at any time in the future for its value at that time.

Dividend revenue is recognized in the period that it is declared. The journal entry for recognition is as follows:

A—Dividends Receivable	XX	
SE—Dividend Revenue		XX

Investments are initially recorded at cost. Subsequently, on the date of the financial statements, the lower of cost and market (LCM) method is used to value the shares. Under the LCM method, the cost of the entire portfolio is compared to its market value on the statement date. If market value is less than cost, an adjusting entry is made to reflect the reduced value of the portfolio.

Learning Tip

For an example of how to apply the LCM method see Exhibit 6-2 on page 323 of the text.

The journal entry to record a reduction in the carrying value of a portfolio is as follows:

SE-Unrealized Loss on Valuation of Temporary Investments	XX	
XA-Valuation Allowance for Temporary Investments		XX

*

Learning Tip

The Unrealized Loss is shown on the income statement; the Allowance account is a contra-account to the Temporary Investments account on the balance sheet.

Unrealized losses are not allowable deductions for income tax purposes.

If, at the end of a subsequent reporting period, the market value of the portfolio has recovered, the reporting entity is allowed to recognize a recovery of the unrealized loss up to the amount of the original cost. The journal entry to record a recovery is as follows:

XA-Valuation Allowance for Temporary Investments	XX	
SE-Recovery of Unrealized Loss on Valuation of Temporary Investments		XX

Learning Tip

The recovery is treated as an unrealized gain on the income statement. Such gains are not recognized for income tax purposes.

The sale of a marketable equity security from the portfolio of temporary investments will usually result in a realized gain or loss because the selling price of the share will differ from its original cost. The journal entries to record a realized gain and loss are as follows:

A realized gain

A—Cash	XX	
A—Temporary Investments		XX
SE—Realized Gain on Sale of Temporary Investments		XX

A realized loss

A—Cash	XX	
SE—Realized Loss on Sale of Temporary Investments	XX	
A—Temporary Investments		XX

Learning Tip

For an example of how both realized and unrealized gains and losses are reported see Exhibit 6-3 on page 325 of the text.

Detailed disclosure of the effects of transactions in marketable security will appear in the financial statement footnotes only if the amounts are significant.

3. Understand how accounts receivable are recognized, valued, recorded, and reported. (pp. 329–336)

The ownership, or right to use, criterion is met by a formal or informal contractual agreement between a firm and its customers. The probable future value criterion is met by the firm's right to receive payment on the accounts in the future.

Under GAAP, accounts receivable must be valued at the present value of the future cash payments on the receivable less allowances for uncollectibles, returns, and discounts. However, due to the short period of time between sales and the collection of receivables, the difference between the gross payments at historical value and present value is considered to be immaterial. As a result, most companies value their accounts receivable at the amount of gross payments due less any allowances.

Adjustment for uncollectibles can be prepared using either the direct write-off method or the allowance method. The direct write-off method recognizes a loss from an uncollectible account in the period in which the account is deemed to be uncollectible. The bad debt policy of the company outlines when an account is to be treated as uncollectible. The journal entry to record an uncollectible account under the direct write-off method is as follows:

SE—Bad Debt Expense	XX	
A—Accounts Receivable (customer's name)		XX

*

Learning Tip

The credit portion of the entry is recorded in the general ledger account (Accounts Receivable) and in the customer's account which is kept in the Accounts Receivable Subsidiary Ledger.

This method violates the matching principle. However, if the write-offs are immaterial, the violation can be ignored.

The allowance method estimates the amount of uncollectible accounts each period and recognizes the related bad debt expense in the same period as the revenues that the receivables helped to generate. The journal entry to record bad debt expense is as follows:

SE—Bad Debt Expense	XX	
XA—Allowance for Doubtful Accounts		XX

Learning Tip

The Allowance for Doubtful Accounts is a contra account to Accounts Receivable and is shown on the balance sheet as a reduction of Accounts Receivable. The resulting amount is called the net realizable value of the receivables.

An account is written off as uncollectible on the date specified by the write-off policy of the firm. The journal entry is as follows:

XA—Allowance for Doubtful Accounts	XX	
A—Accounts Receivable (customer's name)		XX

If an account that has been previously written off is subsequently collected, two journal entries must be made to reflect the transaction: first, the reinstatement of the account and second the collection of it. The entries are as follows:

A—Accounts Receivable (customer's name)	XX	
XA—Allowance for Doubtful Accounts		XX

A—Cash	XX	
A—Accounts Receivable (customer's name)		XX

Learning Tip

For an example of how the allowance method is applied see Exhibit 6-5 on page 335 of the text.

Most companies report accounts receivable net of the allowance for doubtful accounts on the balance sheet.

Two methods can be used to estimate the uncollectible amount for each period: the percentage of credit sales method and the ageing of accounts receivable method. The percentage of credit sales method estimates bad debt expense as follows:

Bad debt expense = Credit sales x Appropriate percentage

The percentage is based on the firm's historical experience or, if the firm is in its first year of operations, on the experience of other firms within the same industry. The percentage is adjusted from time to time based on the collection experience ot the firm.

Discussion of the aging of accounts receivable method is left to intermediate accounting courses.

A firm can generate immediate cash inflow from its receivables either by selling (factoring) them or by borrowing money and using the receivables as collateral (pledging). Under either option the firm will receive less than the face value of the receivables.

If accounts receivable are sold or factored with recourse, the lender can collect the debt from the firm if the debtor defaults on the receivable.

4. Be familiar with the recognition, valuation, recording, and reporting of notes receivable. (pp. 336–339)

The recognition criteria and valuation methods for notes receivable are the same as for accounts receivable; however, a note receivable is evidenced by a formal agreement called a promissory note. This note may show the interest explicitly or implicitly.

If interest is *explicit*, the interest rate will be stated on the face of the note. Interest expense is calculated as follows:

Interest expense = Principal x Interest rate x Time

Although banks and other creditors calculate interest based on the exact number of days that the loan has been outstanding, for ease of calculation most accounting textbooks adopt the convention that each year is made up of 360 days (each month is deemed to have 30 days).

Learning Tip

Principal is the amount of money received by the maker of the note and is also known as the face value of the note.

If interest is implied on the note, the maker actually receives less than the face value of the note. The difference between the face value and the amount received is the implicit interest.

Notes may be issued with collateral (secured notes) or without collateral (unsecured notes). In addition, notes may be sold (factored) or used as collateral to secure a loan.

5. Be aware of how cash, accounts receivable, and temporary investment contribute to financial statement analysis. (pp. 339–343)

The only concerns about cash affecting financial statement analysis arise from cash being restricted, or set aside, due to compensating balances being required by a firm's bank or because management has plans for internal expansion.

Unrealized gains or losses on the current portfolio of equity securities carried at LCM are recognized on the income statement and need to be considered when analyzing any ratio using net income. Unrecorded gains on equity securities could cause some ratios based on net income to be misleading. Information on these amounts could be found in the footnotes.

Short-term liquidity ratios include the *current ratio*, the *quick ratio*, and the *accounts receivable turnover ratio*.

The current ratio is a measure of the extent to which current assets can cover, or pay, current liabilities within the operating cycle. Although the size of this ratio will vary among firms and industries, one rule of thumb is that a safe current ratio is one in which current assets are twice as large as current liabilities; that is, 2:1. The ratio is calculated as follows:

$$\text{Current Ratio} = \frac{\text{Current Assets}}{\text{Current Liabilities}}$$

Some current assets are less liquid than others: for example, inventory must be sold and recorded as accounts receivable before it can be turned into cash; and prepaid expenses are not normally turned into cash at all since they represent services which are due to the firm. This fact may render the current ratio ineffective as a measure of liquidity. To compensate for this problem, the quick ratio eliminates less-liquid current assets from the calculation.

$$\text{Quick Ratio} = \frac{\text{Current Assets} - \text{Inventory}}{\text{Current Liabilities}}$$

One measure of liquidity is the rate at which a firm collects its accounts receivable. The *accounts receivable turnover ratio* should be based on trade accounts receivables only and should exclude financing receivables. The turnover ratio is a measure of how many times the accounts receivable are turned into cash during the year. This ratio and the *number of days'* sales in accounts receivable are both measures of the effectiveness of management's credit granting policies.

$$\text{Accounts Receivable Turnover} = \frac{\text{Total Sales Revenue}}{\text{Average Accounts Receivable}}$$

$$\text{Number of Days' Sales} = \frac{\text{Ending Accounts Receivable}}{\text{Total Sales }/365\text{ days}}$$

Accounts receivable or credit granting policies can be evaluated in other ways as well. A ratio of the amount of accounts receivable written off to the accounts receivable balance over time could indicate the quality of the receivables. In addition, the ratio of the ending balance in the allowance for doubtful accounts to the ending balance in accounts receivable balance would indicate what percentage of the receivables is considered uncollectible.

SELF STUDY

MATCHING

Match the key term to the best explanation.

Key Terms

A. Matching principle
B. Allowance method
C. Collateral
D. Direct write-off method
E. Factoring
F. Percentage of credit sales method
G. Pledging
H. Promissory note
I. Purchasing power
J. Realized gain/loss
K. Recourse
L. Recovery
M. Unrealized gain/loss
N. Valuation allowance
O. Write-off

Explanations

1. __A gain/loss resulting from the sale of an asset.
2. __One method employed in estimating the amount of accounts receivable that may become uncollectible.
3. __The direct write-off method violates this principle under GAAP.
4. __An unrealized gain from revaluing the portfolio of marketable securities under the LCM method.
5. __Selling the accounts receivable of a firm.
6. __A gain/loss recognized in the financial statements that has not resulted in the receipt of cash or a right to receive cash.
7. __A method of valuing accounts receivable based on estimating the amount of future uncollectible accounts.
8. __Using accounts receivable collections to repay a note.
9. __When an account receivable is removed from a firm's books because it is deemed to be uncollectible.
10. __When the buyer of accounts receivable has the right to return a receivable to the seller if the account cannot be collected.
11. __Something of value that is pledged against a debt.
12. __A document in which the issuer agrees to pay the holder fixed amounts at some point in the future.
13. __An account used to reduce the carrying value of the temporary investments account under the LCM method.
14. __A method that recognizes bad debt expense when an account is deemed to be uncollectible.
15. __An attribute of an asset that measures its ability to be exchanged for goods and services.

ASSESS YOUR RECALL

1. Explain how domestic and foreign currencies are measured under GAAP.

2. Explain how marketable equity securities are valued under GAAP.

3. Describe the difference between realized gains/losses and unrealized gains/losses for marketable equity securities.

4. Explain why the direct write-off method violates the matching principle and the allowance method does not.

5. Describe the difference between the theoretical and the practical considerations in the valuation of accounts receivable.

6. Explain how both explicit and implicit interest are calculated.

APPLYING YOUR KNOWLEDGE

1. Kitchener Limited prepares financial statements every quarter. During 19X3, Kitchener entered into the following transactions.

April 1	Purchased 100 shares of Alpha, Inc for $18,000 and 400 shares of Beta Co. for $9,000.
May 15	Beta Co. declared a $0.50/share dividend, payable on June 1.
June 30	Market values: Alpha—$182/share; Beta—$20/share.
July 10	Sold the Beta shares for $8,400.
Aug 5	Purchased 200 shares of Delta Corp. for $9,600.
Sept 30	Market values: Alpha—$183/share; Delta—$46/share.
Oct 7	Purchased 800 shares of Epsilon, Inc. for $12,000.
Nov 12	Sold 80 shares of Alpha for $15,000.
Dec 31	Market values: Alpha—$183/share; Delta—$47/share; Epsilon—$16/share.

a. Prepare the journal entries for 19X3.
b. Show how the transactions affect the 19X3 financial statements.

2. Waterloo Mfg. Limited prepares annual financial statements on December 31. During 19X3 and 19X4, Waterloo entered into the following transactions on its temporary investments.

Apr 2	Purchased 2,000 shares of Omega, Inc. for $40,000.
May 1	Purchased 1,000 shares of Tau Corp. for $7,000.
Aug 1	Omega declared a $1.00/share dividend; payable on August 15.
Dec 31	Market values: Omega—$19/share; Tau—$8/share.
June 30	Sold 500 shares of Omega for $19.50/share.
Oct 3	Sold 200 shares of Tau for $8.50/share.
Dec 31	Market values: Omega—$20/share; Tau—$9/share.

a. Prepare the journal entries for 19X3 and 19X4.
b. Show how the transactions affected financial statements in both years.

Omega => 2000 shares MV 38000 − 2000
=> $40,000
=> sold 500 shares = $9750
Tau Corp => 1000 shares MV 8000 + 1000
=> $7000
=> sold 200
[illegible] $/share

Loss 1000

Cash 9750
Loss 250
ST 10000

Cash 1700

ST 1400
Gain 300

1600

+ 1600

MV 7200 +
Tau → $9 C 5600

600 (+600)

Omega → 20 MV 30000
C 30500
27000

3. The books of a retail sales company revealed the following information for a current period.

Credit sales	$630,000
Accounts receivable balance	64,400
Allowance for doubtful accounts balance	1,500

Assumption for estimating bad debt expense:	
Percentage of credit sales	.5%

a. Prepare the journal entry to record bad debt expense using the percentage of credit sales method.

b. Assume Bill Smits, a customer whose account was previously written off as uncollectible, pays his $50 account. Prepare the journal entry(ies) to record this event.

c. Assume that the account of George Wills in the amount of $120 is deemed to be uncollectible.
Prepare the journal entry to record this event.

SOLUTIONS TO CHAPTER 6

MATCHING

1. J	6. M	11. C
2. F	7. B	12. H
3. A	8. G	13. N
4. L	9. O	14. D
5. E	10. K	15. I

ASSESS YOUR RECALL

1. Domestic currency is valued at its face value under the unit of measure assumption. Foreign currency must be converted to Canadian dollars using the exchange rate on the date of the financial statements. Differences in the exchange rate between statement dates may result in a foreign currency translation gain or loss.

2. Marketable equity securities in a temporary investment portfolio are initially valued at cost. Subsequently, they are valued using the LCM method. Under this method the carrying value of the portfolio is reduced when market value of the portfolio is less than its cost. The resulting unrealized loss is reported on the income statement.

3. Realized gains or losses are the result of the sale of equity securities. The gains or losses are reported on the income statement and are a part of earnings for the period.

Unrealized gains or losses are the result of applying the LCM method and result when the market value of the portfolio is less than its cost. They are also reported on the income statement.

4. The matching principle requires that expenses be recognized in the same period as the revenues that they helped to generate. The direct write-off method recognizes bad debt expense only when an account is considered uncollectible. This may or may not occur in the same period as that in which the revenue is recognized.

The allowance method estimates bad debt expense in the same period in which the revenue that it helped to generate is recognized.

5. The theoretically superior valuation of accounts receivable is the present value of the future cash payments on those receivables less any allowances for uncollectibles, returns, and discounts.

The short period of time between sale and collection leads to the practical valuation used by most companies. Receivables are usually valued at the amount of their gross payments less allowances for uncollectibles. In most cases, allowances for returns and discounts are deemed to be immaterial and, therefore, ignored.

6. Explicit interest is calculated using the interest rate stated on the face of the note. The equation is:

Interest expense = Principal x Interest rate x Time.

Implicit interest is calculated by subtracting the amount of cash received from the face value of the note (the amount to be repaid).

APPLYING YOUR KNOWLEDGE

1. a.

Apr 1	A—	Temporary Investments	27,000	
		A—Cash		27,000
May 15	A—	Dividends Receivable	200	
		SE—Dividend Revenue		200
June 1	A—	Cash	200	
		A—Dividends Receivable		200
June 30	SE—	Unrealized Loss on Valuation of Temporary Investments	800	
		XA—Valuation Allowance for Temporary Investments		800
July 10	A—	Cash	8,400	
		SE-Realized Loss on Sale of Temporary Investments	600	
		A—Temporary Investments		9,000
Aug 5	A—	Temporary Investments	9,600	
		A—Cash		9,600
Sept 30	XA—	Valuation Allowance for Temporary Investments	700	
		OE—Recovery of Unrealized Loss on Valuation of Temporary Investments		700
Oct 7	A—	Temporary Investments	12,000	
		A—Cash		12,000

* Nov	12	A— Cash	15,000	
		A— Temporary Investments		14,400
		SE—Realized Gain on Sale of Temporary Investments		600
* Dec	31:	XA—Valuation Allowance for Temporary Investments	100	
		SE—Recovery of Unrealized Loss on Valuation of Temporary Investments		100

b.

Income Statement:	2nd Qtr	3rd Qtr	4th Qtr
Dividend revenue	$ 200	$ 0	$ 0
Unrealized loss on valuation of TI	(800)	0	0
Realized gain (loss) on sale of TI	0	(600)	600
Recovery of unrealized loss on valuation of TI	0	700	100
Effect on net inc.	$ (600)	$ 100	$ 700

Balance Sheet:			
Temporary Investments at cost	$ 27,000	$ 27,600	$ 25,200
Less Valuation Allowance	(800)	(100)	0
Temp In at LCM	$ 26,200	$ 27,500	$ 25,200

2. a.

Apr	2	A—Temporary Investments	40,000	
		A—Cash		40,000
May	1	A—Temporary Investments	7,000	
		A—Cash		7,000
Aug	1	A—Dividends Receivable	2,000	
		SE—Dividend Revenue		2,000
Aug	15	A—Cash	2,000	
		A—Dividends Receivable		2,000
Dec	31	SE—Unrealized Losses on Temporary Investment	1,000	
		XA—Valuation Allowance for TI		1,000
June	30	A—Cash	9,750	
		SE-Realized Loss on Sale of TI	250	
		A—Temporary Investment		10,000

Oct 3	A—Cash	1,700	
	A—Temporary Investment		1,400
	SE—Realized Gain on Sale of TI		300
Dec 31	XA—Valuation Allowance for TI	1,000	
	SE—Recovery of Unrealized Loss on Temporary Investment		1,000

b.

Income Statement:	19X3	19X4
Dividend revenue	$2,000	$ 0
Unrealized loss on TI		
Recovery of unrealized loss	(1,000)	1,000
Realized gain (loss) on sale of TI	0	50
Effect on net inc.	$1,000	$1,050

Balance Sheet:		
Assets:		
Temporary Investments	$47,000	$35,600
Less Valuation allowance	1,000	0
Temporary Investments (at LCM)	$46,000	$35,600

3 a.

SE—Bad Debt Expense	3,150	
XA—Allowance for Doubtful Accounts		3,150
(630,000 x .005)		

b.

A—Accounts Receivable (Bill Smits)	50	
XA—Allowance for Doubtful Accounts		50
A—Cash	50	
A—Accounts Receivable (Bill Smits)		50

c.

SE—Allowance for Doubtful Accounts	120	
A—Accounts Receivable (George Wills)		120

CHAPTER 7

INVENTORY

CHAPTER OVERVIEW

This chapter outlines the valuation and reporting alternatives for inventory. Like marketable securities, inventory is valued at the lower of cost and market (LCM) at each financial statement reporting date. Note, however, that the application of the LCM rule differs somewhat for inventory. For example, when market is lower than cost and inventory is written down, the write-down is considered permanent.

The accounting systems that track inventory costs during the year are called the cost inventory systems. Two such systems are outlined in the chapter—the periodic system and the perpetual system. Under a periodic system the cost of goods sold and the ending inventory balances are determined by taking a physical count of the inventory at the end of the period. In contrast, under a perpetual system the cost of goods sold and inventory balances are maintained on a day-to-day basis.

Regardless of the inventory cost system in use, cost is assigned to the cost of goods sold and the ending inventory by means of one of four alternative cost flow assumptions: specific identification, first-in, first-out (FIFO), last-in, first-out (LIFO), and weighted average. The specific identification assumption requires that items in inventory be tracked individually. Under the FIFO assumption, the most recent costs are assigned to ending inventory while under the LIFO assumption, the oldest costs are assigned to ending inventory. Under the weighted average assumption the average unit cost is assigned to ending inventory.

LIFO and FIFO produce significantly different results in periods of changing prices. LIFO will produce the lowest income in periods of rising prices.

LEARNING OBJECTIVES

1. Understand the conceptual basis for the recognition and valuation of inventory.
2. Understand the difference between a periodic inventory system and a perpetual inventory system.
3. Be able to apply each of the cost flow assumptions to ending inventory and cost of goods sold.
4. Understand the factors that constrain the choice of a cost flow assumption.
5. Understand the difference between FIFO and LIFO and how each can affect financial reporting.
6. Be familiar with how inventory can be estimated.
7. Understand how inventories contribute to financial statement analysis.

CHAPTER REVIEW

1. Understand the conceptual basis for the recognition and valuation of inventory. (pp. 367–374)

Inventory meets the ownership, or right to use, criterion either by being in the possession of the firm or by evidence of title to the goods. It meets the probable future value criterion because the firm has the ability to sell the inventory in the future and receive payment in return.

Under GAAP, inventory is initially recorded at acquisition, or laid-down, cost. For a retailer, laid-down cost includes the purchase price of the goods plus all other costs incurred to take possession of the goods and ready them for sale; for example, the costs of ordering, receiving, handling, and inspecting. As a practical matter, if some of the latter costs (for example, freight-in) are immaterial most firms will expense them as they are incurred. For a manufacturer, cost consists of the laid-down costs incurred for direct materials, direct labour, and overhead.

For reporting purposes, inventory is valued at the lower of cost and market (LCM). Although the application of this rule is similar to that for marketable securities in a temporary investments portfolio, there are some significant differences in application. For example, the LCM rule may be applied to individual units in inventory, to pools of similar items, or to the inventory as a whole. Generally, the rule is applied to pools of similar items in inventory. In addition, once an unrealized loss has been recognized on application of the LCM rule, it may not be recovered in a subsequent period.

Under GAAP, market value is defined as either replacement cost or net realizable value (NRV).

Learning Tip

> ✱ Replacement cost, or entry value, is defined as the amount of cash that would be required to acquire similar goods in similar condition today. NRV, or exit value, is defined as selling price minus any costs that would be incurred to complete and sell the item.

When the market value of inventory is less than its cost, the unrealized loss, called a holding loss, is included on the income statement. If the amount is significant, the loss will be disclosed as a separate line item in the income statement or will be discussed in a footnote. If the loss is not significant in amount, it is allowed to flow through to the cost of goods sold.

2. Understand the difference between a periodic inventory system and a perpetual inventory system. (pp. 376–378)

Inventory systems can be designed to keep track of the number of units in inventory (physical inventory systems) or the costs associated with those units (cost inventory systems). The focus in the text is on cost inventory systems.

A perpetual inventory system is designed to account for the cost of goods sold and the inventory balances on a day-to-day basis. Every transaction that affects inventory is recorded by journal entry to the inventory account daily.

Firms that need timely information about their inventories for pricing and ordering decisions will probably use a perpetual inventory system.

Learning Tip

> At least once a year, a physical inventory count should be taken and compared to the inventory account balance. If a difference exists between the book value and the value per the count, it could be a result of inventory shrinkage (that is, a loss due to theft, damage, or spoilage).

Periodic inventory systems do not account for the cost of goods sold or the inventory balances on a daily basis. There are no journal entries posted to the inventory accounts during the year. Transactions affecting inventory are recorded in accounts other than inventory. At the end of a reporting period, a physical inventory count must be taken in order to establish the ending inventory balance. The cost of goods sold is determined by adding the beginning balance in inventory to the purchases for the year. This sum is called the cost of goods available for sale. The ending inventory balance is then subtracted from the cost of goods available for sale to derive the cost of goods sold.

A periodic inventory system is less costly to install and maintain than a perpetual system but the information derived from it is not as timely.

Learning Tip

> The amount of inventory shrinkage cannot be measured with any precision if a periodic inventory system is used. Any items of inventory that are no longer in stock and, therefore, not subject to count are assumed to have been sold.

3. Be able to apply each of the cost flow assumptions to ending inventory and the cost of goods sold. (pp. 378–384)

In order to determine the ending balances in the cost of goods sold and inventory a firm has to adopt one of four different cost flow assumptions:

- specific identification
- first-in, first-out (FIFO)
- last-in, first-out (LIFO)
- weighted average.

Learning Tip

> Under GAAP, a firm is required to choose the method which is the fairest matching of costs with revenues. The cost flow assumption adopted is not necessarily the same as the physical flow of goods.

Specific identification is used by firms that have the need and the ability to keep track of each unit sold and each unit in inventory. This method requires that the goods in inventory be unique; that is, each item can be readily identified. Examples of inventory subject to specific identification would include automobiles, works of art, and precious gems. If this method is chosen, detailed records must be kept for every item in inventory.

Under FIFO, the costs of the first units purchased are assigned to the first units sold. As a result, the cost of goods sold contains the oldest costs and the ending inventory, the most recent costs. An acronym often used for the ending inventory under FIFO is last-in, still- here (LISH).

Learning Tip

For a numeric example see Exhibits 7-7 and 7-8 on pages 379 and 380 of the text.

Under LIFO, the costs of the most recent units purchased are assigned to first units sold. The cost of goods sold contains the most recent costs and the ending inventory, the oldest costs. An acronym for the ending inventory under LIFO is first-in, still-here (FISH).

Learning Tip

For a graphic example see Exhibit 7-9 on page 381 of the text.

Under the weighted average method an average cost of inventory on hand during the period is calculated. This average is then applied to units in both the cost of goods sold and ending inventory. The average cost is calculated by dividing the cost of goods available for sale (beginning inventory plus purchases) by the number of units available for sale.

Learning Tip

The weighted average method produces a dollar value for the cost of goods sold and ending inventory that is midway between the values assigned by FIFO and LIFO. For a graphic example see Exhibit 7-10 on page 383 of the text.

4. Understand the factors that constrain the choice of a cost flow assumption. (pp. 384–387)

As stated previously, under GAAP, the reporting entity must choose the cost flow assumption that best reflects a fair matching of costs to revenues during the period. A complicating factor in this decision is the fact that the FIFO and LIFO cost flow assumptions produce significantly different results whenever prices are changing. This, in turn, can result in significantly different reported income under FIFO versus LIFO.

Learning Tip

When prices are stable, FIFO, LIFO, and weighted average will all produce the same cost of goods sold and inventory balances.

5. Understand the difference between FIFO and LIFO and how each can affect financial reporting.

In periods of rising prices, net income under LIFO will be lower than net income under FIFO. Under LIFO, gross profit results from matching the most recent costs of inventory against current revenues. Under FIFO, on the other hand, the oldest inventory costs are matched against current revenues. As a result, under FIFO gross profit contains both a current gross profit (current revenue minus current costs) and a realized holding gain (current cost minus historical cost).

Learning Tip

For numeric examples see Exhibits 7-11 and 7-12 on pages 384 and 385 of the text.

Ending inventory under LIFO reflects the oldest prices incurred by a firm. These costs may go back to a firm's first year of operations. The cumulative difference between those original prices and current prices could be significant.

Revenue Canada does not allow the use of LIFO for income tax purposes. As a result, there are relatively few Canadian corporations using the LIFO cost flow assumption. The cost of using one method for financial reporting and one for income tax reporting is prohibitive. In addition, during periods of rising prices, there is no advantage to using LIFO (which would produce a lower net income) for financial reporting and FIFO (which would produce a higher net income) for income tax reporting.

6. Be familiar with how inventory balances can be estimated. (pp. 387 -388)

A company using a periodic inventory system may wish to produce interim financial statements. If the company is unwilling or unable to count its inventory mid-year, it will need a reliable method to estimate the cost of goods sold and the inventory. The same need would exist if the inventory were destroyed by a disaster or stolen. One method to do so is called the **gross margin estimation** method. Using this method, sales are multiplied by the normal gross margin percentage (gross margin/sales) to arrive at gross margin. Sales minus gross margin equals the cost of goods sold. If the cost of goods sold is subtracted from goods available for sale, the result is the estimated cost of ending inventory. To use this method, a company must have a historically consistent gross margin percentage.

Gross margin percentage = Gross margin/Sales

Beginning inventory + Purchases = Goods available for sale

Sales—Gross margin = Cost of goods sold

Goods available for sale—Cost of goods sold = Ending inventory

7. Understand how inventories contribute to financial statement analysis. (pp. 388–390)

Cross-industry analysis of inventory ratios is difficult to perform because of the different cost flow assumptions in use by different firms. As demonstrated earlier, the cost flow assumptions can produce significantly different results in the financial statements. In order to make comparisons across firms, the user must take the differences among methods into account. In analyzing the reporting entity itself, the user should compare the ratios over a period of time to determine if there are any trends that should be noted in the performance of the company.

Inventory turnover measures how often a company sells and replaces its inventory. As a rule, a company should turn its inventory often enough that it is not incurring the cost of carrying excess stock in inventory but not so often that it cannot meet orders from its customers. The inventory turnover is calculated as follows:

Inventory turnover = Cost of goods sold/Average inventory

A related ratio is the number of days that inventory is held. The number of days in inventory is calculated as follows:

Number of days in inventory = 365/Inventory turnover

SELF STUDY

MATCHING

Match the key term to the best explanation.

Key Terms

A. Current gross margin
B. Entry market
C. Exit market
D. FIFO
E. Goods available for sale
F. Inventory shrinkage
G. LIFO
H. Laid-down cost
I. Gross margin estimation method
J. Specific identification
K. Net realizable value
L. Periodic inventory system
M. Perpetual inventory system
N. Replacement cost
O. Weighted average costing

Explanations

1. ___ Beginning inventory plus purchases.
2. ___ Invoice price + customs duties, freight, insurance cost, etc.
3. ___ The current price at which a unit of inventory could be purchased by a firm.
4. ___ Current selling price minus current replacement cost.
5. ___ Selling price less any costs necessary to complete and sell a unit.
6. ___ Based on dividing the cost of goods available for sale by the number of units available for sale.
7. ___ A system in which the cost of goods sold is determined when a unit is sold.
8. ___ A cost flow assumption in which the ending inventory consists of the most recent inventory costs.
9. ___ The market from which goods are purchased by a firm.
10. ___ Cost flow assumption used where goods in inventory are unique and where the unit cost of each item can be determined at any time.
11. ___ The loss of inventory due to theft, spoilage, and damage.
12. ___ The use of a cost-to-sales ratio to estimate ending inventory.
13. ___ A system in which the cost of goods sold is derived at the end of an accounting period.
14. ___ The cost flow assumption in which the ending inventory consists of the oldest inventory costs.
15. ___ The market in which a firm sells its goods.

ASSESS YOUR RECALL

1. Identify two ways that the application of the LCM rule differs between marketable equity securities in a temporary investments portfolio and inventory.

2. Explain how market value is determined under the LCM rule.

3. Identify and define the three major cost flow assumptions.

4. Explain why physical inventory counts are necessary under both the periodic and the perpetual inventory systems.

APPLYING YOUR KNOWLEDGE

1. Banner, Inc. applies the LCM rule to its inventory on a pool basis. Shown below are data taken from each of the firm's four inventory pools on a per unit basis:

Pool	Original Cost	Replacement Cost	NRV
1	$70	$72	$76
2	94	90	95
3	90	88	87
4	90	87	90

Determine the per unit valuation to be used for each pool under the LCM rule.

2. The following data apply to the merchandise inventory of Cambridge Company Limited for the month of August.

	Units	Unit Cost	
8/ 1	Beginning inventory	1,000	$3
8/ 6	Sale	500	
8/12	Purchase	2,000	4
8/18	Sale	1,000	
8/24	Purchase	500	6
8/30	Sale	1,900	

sell to total 3400.

Compute the cost of goods sold and ending inventory on August 31 under each of the following cost assumptions.

a. FIFO, periodic

b. FIFO, perpetual

c. LIFO, periodic

d. LIFO, perpetual

e. weighted average, periodic

f. weighted average, perpetual

FIFO = 3 × 1000
4 × 2000
6 × 4000
3400 units
⇓
avail to sell.

3400 ⇒ sold

500
2000
3400
900 ⇒ units beg inv

900×3 = 2700.

2700 + 8000 +
↓
(2000×4)
6×500
3×900

3. The following data pertain to the merchandise inventory of Jamul, Inc. The replacement cost per unit is $40.

	Unit	Unit Cost	Unit Sales Price
Beginning inventory	400	$20	
Purchases	600	30	
Sales	500		$50

a. Prepare an abbreviated income statement showing sales, cost of goods sold, and gross margin under both LIFO and FIFO.
b. Show how the FIFO gross margin can be divided into a current gross margin and a realized holding gain.
c. Compute the unrealized holding gains under both FIFO and LIFO.

4. Gardner Limited began operations at the beginning of 19X8. At the end of 19X9, management wants to determine what the effects of alternative inventory costing methods would have been on the income and financial position of the company. Consider the following data.

	19X8	19X9
Sales	$1,300	$1,200
Purchases	1,100	900
Ending inventory:		
LIFO	305	400
FIFO	288	370

a. Which inventory method would yield a higher net income for 19X8?

b. Which inventory method would yield a higher net income for 19X9?

c. Which inventory method would result in a higher total of assets at the end of 19X9?

d. Which inventory method would result in a higher dollar amount of purchases for 19X9?

e. Which inventory method would result in a higher total in shareholders' equity at the end of 19X9?

f. During 19X9 were inventory prices rising or falling?

SOLUTIONS TO CHAPTER 7

MATCHING

1. E	6. O	11. F
2. H	7. M	12. I
3. N	8. D	13. L
4. A	9. B	14. G
5. K	10. J	15. C

ASSESS YOUR RECALL

1. The LCM rule is applied to marketable equity securities on a portfolio basis. For inventory, however, it can be applied to individual items, to pools of similar items, or to the inventory as a whole.

The definition of market for marketable equity securities is the net realizable value (selling price) of the entire portfolio. For inventory, market is defined as either replacement cost or net realizable value.

2. Replacement cost (entry value) is the amount of cash that would be required to acquire similar goods in similar condition today. Net realizable value (exit value) is the anticipated selling price of the goods minus the costs required to complete and sell the items.

3. FIFO (first-in, first-out)—the costs of the first units purchased are assigned to the first units sold. Under this assumption, the cost of goods sold contains the oldest costs while ending inventory contains the recent costs.

LIFO (last-in, first-out)—the costs of the most recent purchases are assigned to the first units sold. Under this assumption the cost of goods sold contains the most recent costs while ending inventory contains the oldest costs.

Weighted average—the average cost of the goods available for sale are assigned to both the cost of goods sold and ending inventory.

4. Physical inventory counts are necessary under periodic systems because they establish the ending inventory value and allow for the determination of the cost of goods sold.

Perpetual systems require physical inventory counts to prove the validity of the inventory account balance and to establish whether or not inventory shrinkage has occurred.

APPLYING YOUR KNOWLEDGE

1.

Original Cost	Replacement Cost	NRV	LCM
$ 70	$ 72	$ 76	$70
94	90	95	90
90	88	87	87
90	87	90	87

2.

	Units	Total cost	
a. Beginning inventory	1,000	$ 3,000	sell 1st
Purchases	2,500	11,000	
Available	3,500	14,000	
Less: Sales	3,400	13,400	Cost of goods sold
Ending inventory	100	$ 600	

or 100 units x $6 = $600

b.

	Purchased			Sold			Balance		
Date	Units	$per Unit	Total $	Units	$per Unit	Total $	Units	$per Unit	Total $
8/ 1							1,000	3	3,000
– 6				500	3	1,500	500	3	1,500
– 12	2,000	4	8,000				500	3	1,500
							2,000	4	8,000
							2,500		9,500
– 18				500	3	1,500	1,500	4	6,000
				500	4	2,000			
				1,000		3,500			
– 24	500	6	3,000				1,500	4	6,000
							500	6	3,000
							2,000		9,000

	Purchased			Sold			Balance		
Date	Units	$per Unit	Total $	Units	$per Unit	Total $	Units	$per Unit	Total $
– 30				1,500	4	6,000	100	6	600
				400	6	2,400			
				1,900		8,400			
Ending inventory							100	6	600
Cost of goods sold				3,400		13,400			

c.

	Units	Total cost	
Beginning inventory	1,000	$ 3,000	
Purchases	2,500	11,000	
Available	3,500	14,000	
Less: Sales	3,400	13,700	Cost of goods sold
Ending inventory	100	$ 300	

or 100 units x $3 = $300

d.

	Purchased			Sold			Balance		
Date	Units	$per Unit	Total $	Units	$per Unit	Total $	Units	$per Unit	Total $
8/1							1,000	3	3,000
6				500	3	1,500	500	3	1,500
12	2,000	4	8,000				500	3	1,500
							2,000	4	8,000
							2,500		9,500
18				1,000	4	4,000	500	3	1,500
							1,000	4	4,000
							1,500		5,500
24	500	6	3,000				500	3	1,500
							1,000	4	4,000
							500	6	3,000
							2,000		8,500
30				500	6	3,000	100	3	300
				1,000	4	4,000			
				400	3	1,200			
				1,900		8,200			
Ending inventory							100	3	300
Cost of goods sold				3,400		13,700			

e. Cost of goods available = $3,000 + 8,000 + 3,000 = $14,000
No. of units available = 1,000 + 2,000 + 500 = 3,500
Ave. cost per unit = $14,000/3,500 = $4.00/unit
Ending inventory = 100 units x $4 = $400
Cost of goods sold = 3,400 units x $4 = $13,600

f.

	Purchased			Sold			Balance		
Date	Units	$per Unit	Total$	Units	$per Unit	Total$	Units	$per Unit	Total$
8/ 1							1,000	3	3,000
– 6				500	3	1,500	500	3	1,500
– 12	2,000	4	8,000				500	3	1,500
							2,000	4	8,000
							2,500	3.80	9,500
– 18				1,000	3.80	3,800	1,500	3.80	5,700
– 24	500	6	3,000				1,500	3.80	5,700
							500	6.00	3,000
							2,000	4.35	8,700
– 30				1,900	4.35	8,265	100	4.35	435
Ending inventory							100	4.35	435
Cost of goods sold				3,400		13,565			

3.

a. **LIFO**	Units	Cost/Unit	Total Cost
Sales	500	$50	$25,000
Cost of goods sold	500	30	15,000
Gross margin			$10,000
FIFO			
Sales	500	$50	$25,000
Cost of goods sold	400	20	8,000
	100	30	3,000
	500		11,000
Gross margin			$14,000

b. **FIFO**

Sales	500	$50	$25,000

Replacement CGS	500	40	20,000
Current gross margin			5,000
Realized holding gain*			9,000
Gross margin			$14,000

*Replacement CGS–Historical CGS: 20,000–11,000 = 9,000

c.

	FIFO	LIFO
Ending inventory @ replacement cost	$20,000	$20,000
Ending inventory @ historical cost	15,000	11,000
Unrealized holding gain	$ 5,000	$ 9,000

4. a. Net income is higher using LIFO since it results in a lower value for the cost of goods sold.

	FIFO	LIFO
Beginning inventory (BI)	-	-
Purchases (P)	1,100	1,100
Goods available (GA)	1,100	1,100
Ending inventory (EI)	(288)	(305)
Cost of goods sold (CGS)	812	795

b. Net income is higher using LIFO since the cost of goods sold is lower.

	FIFO	LIFO
BI	288	305
P	900	900
GA	1,188	1,205
EI	(370)	(400)
CGS	818	805

c. LIFO results in a higher ending inventory; therefore, total assets are higher under LIFO.

d. The dollar amount of purchases is the same for both LIFO and FIFO.

e. LIFO, since net income is higher using LIFO in both 19X8 and 19X9.

f. Prices were falling. FIFO values for inventory are close to market (last-in, still-here). Ending inventory under FIFO is lower than LIFO in both years.

CHAPTER 8

CAPITAL ASSETS

CHAPTER OVERVIEW

This chapter outlines the recognition, valuation, and recording of capital assets. The assets discussed include property, plant, and equipment, natural resources, and intangible assets. Capital assets are initially recorded at acquisition cost. Acquisition cost includes all costs necessary to acquire the asset and prepare it for its intended use. In the case of self-constructed assets, cost could include interest during the construction period.

Subsequent to acquisition, the cost of capital assets other than land must be allocated to the periods in which the benefits from the assets are received. This allocation, called amortization, must be both systematic and rational. The amortization of natural resources is often referred to as depletion.

Amortization for financial reporting purposes can be calculated using the straight line method, accelerated methods, or production methods. For income tax reporting, Revenue Canada requires that assets be amortized using Capital Cost Allowance (CCA) methods. The calculation of amortization for financial reporting can differ significantly from the calculation of CCA for income tax reporting. This means that income tax expense, which is based on financial statement income, and income taxes payable, which is based on taxable income, can differ significantly as well. The difference between income tax expense, per the financial statements, and income taxes payable, per the tax return, is referred to as deferred income taxes.

A firm involved in oil exploration can choose between capitalizing all developmental costs (full costing) or capitalizing only the costs of successful projects (successful efforts). The most common method of amortizing the cost of a natural resource is the units of production method.

Intangible assets have no physical form. They derive their benefits from the fact that they confer rights to the firm; for example, a patent allows a company exclusive right to manufacture a product or use a process. An intangible asset may be capitalized only if the asset has been purchased from a third party. With the exception of some development costs, the costs of generating an intangible asset internally must be expensed as incurred. The most common method of amortizing the cost of an intangible asset is the straight line method.

LEARNING OBJECTIVES

1. Understand the conceptual basis for the recognition and valuation of capital assets.
2. Understand when GAAP allows the capitalization of interest on self-constructed assets.
3. Be able to calculate amortization for financial reporting purposes.
4. Understand how deferred income taxes come about.
5. Understand how to account for changes in amortization methods as well as changes in estimates.
6. Understand how to account for the disposal or write-off of capital assets.
7. Be able to calculate the amortization of natural resources.
8. Be familiar with the different kinds of intangible assets and how they are amortized.
9. Understand how capital assets contribute to financial statement analysis.

CHAPTER REVIEW

1. Understand the conceptual basis for the recognition and valuation of capital assets. (pp. 413–414)

Capital assets meet the ownership, or right to use, criterion either by being in the possession of the firm or by evidence of legal title to the assets. The assets meet the probable future value criterion by virtue of the fact that they will generate cash from future revenues or from their future sale.

Property, plant, and equipment (PPE) is valued at its acquisition cost. This includes all costs necessary to acquire the asset and prepare it for its intended use. Acquisition cost could include invoice price (less any discounts), transportation-in, installation costs, taxes, legal fees, and interest (for self-constructed assets). A decline in value is recognized only if the asset has been seriously and permanently impaired.

Occasionally acquisition cost must be apportioned amongst several assets that were acquired for a single price (a basket purchase). A portion of the purchase price is allocated to each asset based on the fair market value of each asset relative to the fair market of the basket purchase as a whole.

Learning Tip

For a numeric example see page 417 of the text.

Natural resources, such as oil exploration, are recorded using either the full cost method or the successful efforts method. The former capitalizes the full costs of all projects—both successes and failures. The latter method capitalizes only the costs incurred on successful projects.

Intangible assets are capitalized only if they are acquired from a third party. Costs incurred in generating intangible assets internally are expensed as incurred. One exception to this rule is deferred development costs. Development costs may be capitalized only if the costs meet very strict criteria:

- the product or process must be clearly defined and marketable
- the product or process must be technically feasible
- and the resources must be available to complete the project.

2. Understand when GAAP allows the capitalization of interest on self-constructed assets. (p. 417)

When a firm constructs a capital asset for its own use and borrows the money to fund the construction, the interest costs incurred during the construction period may be capitalized.

Canadian GAAP is silent as to specific guidelines for interest capitalization; however, if the interest costs are directly attributable to self-constructed assets they may be capitalized.

Learning Tip

Remember that only the interest costs incurred during the construction period may be capitalized and then only if they are directly attributable to the self-constructed asset.

3. Be able to calculate amortization for financial reporting purposes. (pp. 419–428)

Amortization is not a measure of the decreased value of a capital asset over time. It is, rather, a systematic and rational allocation of the cost of the asset over its useful life. There are three common methods in use to calculate amortization on tangible capital assets for financial reporting purposes: the straight line method, the accelerated methods such as declining balance, and the production methods.

Learning Tip

Land is a capital asset that is deemed to have indefinite future benefit. As a result, amortization is not charged against it.

Under straight line amortization the original cost of the asset minus its residual value is allocated evenly over its useful life. Residual value and useful life are both estimates made by management. This method is appropriate for those assets that give up their benefits evenly over their useful lives. The formula for annual depreciation under this method is as follows:

$$\text{Amortization expense} = \frac{\text{Original cost} - \text{Residual value}}{\text{Estimated useful life}}$$

The production methods are a variant of the straight line method. They differ from the straight line time method in that output from the asset is defined as usage rather than number of years of life. Amortization is calculated as follows:

$$\text{Amortization expense per unit} = \frac{\text{Cost} - \text{Residual value}}{\text{Estimated total units of output}}$$

Learning Tip

For a numeric example see Exhibit 8-4 on page 423 of the text.

Accelerated methods are applied by multiplying the carrying value of an asset by a fixed percentage. Under the double declining balance method the percentage is determined by doubling the straight line amortization rate. An asset having a five year useful life is amortized at the straight line rate of 1/5, or 20%, per year. The double declining balance rate for the same asset would be 2 x 20%, or 40%, per year.

Annual amortization is calculated by multiplying the asset's book value (cost minus accumulated amortization) by the declining balance rate.

Learning Tip

For a numeric example see Exhibit 8-5 on page 424 of the text.

For each of the amortization methods suitable for financial reporting, the total amount of amortization that can be charged over the life of an asset is equal to the amortizable cost of the asset (original cost – residual value). Under straight line amortization this is accomplished by using the amortizable cost in the annual amortization calculation. Double declining balance does not consider residual value in the calculation of annual amortization. To allow for residual value, the amortization expense in the last year of the asset's life is adjusted to ensure that the total amortization taken over the asset's life matches its amortizable cost.

4. Understand how deferred taxes come about. (pp. 425–428)

The amortization methods used for financial reporting purposes can differ significantly from those used for income tax reporting. Revenue Canada does not allow corporations to deduct accounting amortization expense from taxable income. Instead, Revenue Canada allows a deduction for capital cost allowance (CCA) which could be thought of as amortization for tax reporting purposes. For income tax purposes, capital assets are assigned to various classes which prescribe how CCA for a given asset is to be calculated. The rates and methods prescribed for the asset classes do not necessarily conform to the methods and rates used for financial reporting. In addition, for income tax purposes only one-half of the calculated CCA may be deducted in the year that an asset is acquired. The difference between amortization and CCA is called a timing difference; that is, it will reverse later in an asset's life. As a result there is usually a difference between income tax expense per the financial statements and income taxes payable per the income tax return. The difference between income tax expense (shown on the income statement) and income taxes payable (derived from the tax return) is called deferred tax. Deferred tax represents taxes that may have to be paid later in an asset's life when the timing differences reverse.

Learning Tip

For a numeric example see Exhibit 8-8 on page 427 of the text.

5. Understand how to account for changes in amortization methods as well as changes in estimate. (pp. 428–430)

Amortization for book purposes is based on two estimates–residual value and useful life. Over time, a firm may reevaluate and revise either one or both of these estimates. A change in estimate is accounted for on a prospective basis; that is, there is no recalculation or restatement of the amortization charged in prior periods. The change is made in the current and future periods. The formula to calculate the revised annual depreciation deduction under the straight line method is as follows:

$$\text{Depreciation expense} = \frac{\text{Remaining book value} - \text{Residual value}}{\text{Remaining useful life}}$$

The nature of such a change and its effects on the current year are disclosed in the notes to the financial statements.

Changes in the method of calculating amortization are changes in accounting principle and must be applied retroactively. The cumulative affect of a change in accounting principle must be calculated and disclosed in the income statement and the notes to the financial statements. Comparative figures in the financial statement must be restated.

6. Understand how to account for the disposal or write-off of capital assets. (p. 430)

When an asset is sold both its cost and its accumulated amortization must be removed from the books. The difference between the selling price of the asset and its book value is recognized as a gain or a loss on the sale.

If an asset is deemed to be worthless, its remaining book value is removed from the books. If no cash was received, the amount of the loss is equal to the book value of the asset.

Learning Tip

For a numeric example see the journal entries on page 430 of the text.

7. Be able to calculate the amortization of natural resources. (p. 431)

The most common method used to calculate the amortization, or depletion, of a natural resource is called the units of production method.

The annual amortization expense is calculated by multiplying the cost of the asset by a production ratio. The production ratio is calculated as follows:

$$\text{Production ratio} = \frac{\text{Actual units produced for the period}}{\text{Total estimated units to be produced}}$$

8. Be familiar with the different kinds of intangible assets and how they are amortized. (pp. 431–435)

The cost of intangible assets is capitalized only if the asset is acquired from a third party. The costs associated with internally generated intangible assets are expensed as incurred.

The most common method in use to amortize intangible assets is straight line amortization. Intangible assets are considered to have a residual value of zero. An intangible asset is amortized over the lesser of its useful life or legal life, and 40 years.

Research costs and advertising costs are examples of costs that might be considered to be intangible assets; that is, costs that are incurred because they will generate future revenues. Because it is extremely difficult to measure those benefits and to assign them to future periods, the costs attendant on research or advertising activities are expensed as incurred. The costs of developing research findings into a marketable product may be capitalized if certain criteria are met: the product or process is technically feasible; it has a defined market; management intends to market the product; and resources are available to do so. A firm can, however, capitalize the costs of filing for the registration of patents, trademarks, copyrights, and the like.

Goodwill may exist for a number of reasons: above average earnings ability; excellent management; good location; quality products; or excellent employee and/or customer relationships. Under GAAP, goodwill is recognized only when one firm acquires it by purchasing another firm. It is defined as the excess of the purchase price over the fair value of the net assets acquired. Goodwill is amortized over the lesser of its useful life and 40 years.

9. Understand how capital assets contribute to financial statement analysis. (pp. 435–441)

In comparing the financial statements of two different firms, the users of financial statements should be aware of the fact that the reported results of the firms could differ because different capitalization or amortization policies were adopted by the firms.

Capital assets are recorded at historical cost minus accumulated amortization. Another concern of the user will be whether historical cost is a fair representation of current value—capital assets could be worth considerably more, or less, than their book value.

One measure of how well management has managed the resources of the company is the Return on Assets (ROA) Ratio. This ratio measures return (performance) as a percentage of total assets.

Learning Tip

For a numeric example see the shaded box on page 439 of the text.

SELF STUDY

MATCHING

Match the key term to the best explanation.

Key Terms

A. Accelerated amortization
B. Amortization
C. Basket purchase
D. Book value
E. Deferred tax
F. Depletion
G. Amortizable cost
H. Double declining balance amortization
I. Goodwill
J. Intangible assets
K. Capital cost allowance
L. Residual value
M. Straight line amortization
N. Production methods
O. Useful life

Explanations

1. __Annual amortization of a capital asset based on the assumption that benefits derived from the asset are related to the output or use of the asset.
2. __Capital assets without physical form.
3. __An estimate of the amount a firm believes that it can recover at the end of a capital asset's life.
4. __An account created by the differences between accounting income reported on the financial statements and taxable income reported on the income tax return.
5. __The method that allocates more amortization to an asset's earlier years than the straight-line method does.
6. __Another term for the amortization of the cost of a natural resource.
7. __An amortization method used for income tax reporting purposes.
8. __Used to allocate the cost of capital assets to expense over their economic lives.
9. __An estimate of how long an asset will be of economic value to a firm.
10. __Allocates amortization expense evenly over an asset's useful life.
11. __The difference between the original cost of a capital asset and its accumulated amortization.
12. __An amortization method using a rate that is double the rate used under straight-line.
13. __When more than one asset is acquired for a single purchase price.
14. __Recognized when one firm acquires another for a price that exceeds the fair market value of the net assets acquired.
15. __The original cost of an asset minus its residual value.

ASSESS YOUR RECALL

1. On what type of asset is interest a capitalizable cost? When does interest capitalization begin and end?

2. Define amortization.

3. List the three primary amortization methods and explain how annual amortization is determined under each.

4. Explain how capital cost allowance (CCA) differs from the amortization methods used for financial reporting purposes.

5. Explain the rules for recognizing and amortizing intangible assets.

APPLYING YOUR KNOWLEDGE

1. On June 1, 19X4, Omega, Inc. acquired the following items for $60,000 at an auction: a truck, some equipment, and some tools. The fair market values of these items was $25,200; $45,000; and $19,800, respectively. Prepare the journal entry to record the acquisition.

2. Kurz Co. Ltd. purchased an automobile with a list price of $16,000. The dealer allowed a discount of $900 from the list price because payment was made in cash. Dealer preparation charges on the automobile were $350. The dealer also collected 8% sales tax on the automobile and the preparation charges. Additional costs incurred were $60 for vehicle registration and license plates and $700 for a one-year insurance policy. Kurz paid a body shop $90 for painting the company name on the automobile. Prepare the journal entries to record the transaction.

3. A piece of equipment is purchased on January 1, 19X4 for $30,000. The estimated residual value is $2,000; and the expected useful life is 4 years. Compute the amortization for each year using the following methods.

a. Straight line
b. Double-declining balance (DDB)

4. On January 1, 19X3 a truck is purchased for $50,000. The expected residual value and useful life are $5,000 and 5 years. The company uses straight line amortization. At the beginning of 19X5, the estimated residual value is changed to $8,000 and the useful life extended by 2 years over the original estimate. Determine the amortization expense for 19X3 and 19X5.

SOLUTIONS TO CHAPTER 8

MATCHING

1.	N	6.	F	11.	D
2.	J	7.	K	12.	H
3.	L	8.	B	13.	C
4.	E	9.	O	14.	I
5.	A	10.	M	15.	G

ASSESS YOUR RECALL

1. Interest is capitalizable on self-constructed assets. Capitalizable interest is allowed only between the beginning and completion of the construction period.

2. Amortization is the systematic and rational allocation of the cost of a capital asset over the periods for which the asset is expected to provide economic benefit.

3. a. Straight-line

$$\text{Amortization} = \frac{\text{Original cost} - \text{residual value}}{\text{Estimated useful life}}$$

b. Double declining balance

Amortization = Book value at the beginning of each year x 200% of straight line rate

c. Production methods

$$\text{Amortization per unit} = \frac{\text{Original cost} - \text{residual value}}{\text{estimated total output in units}}$$

In all cases, total accumulated amortization cannot exceed the amortizable cost (original cost − residual value) of the asset.

4. CCA differs from financial reporting amortization in several ways: all assets are grouped into classes as defined by Revenue Canada; each class has a prescribed rate used to calculate the maximum amount that may be deducted; only one-half of the maximum amount may be taken as a deduction in the year the asset is acquired.

5. Intangible assets are capitalized only if they are purchased from an outside third party. Amortization is taken over an asset's useful life, not to exceed 40 years.

APPLYING YOUR KNOWLEDGE

1.

A — Trucks	16,800*	
A — Equipment	30,000*	
A — Tools	13,200*	
A–Cash		60,000

Asset	FMV	Percentage			* Allocation
Truck	$25,200	25,200/90,000	=	28%	60,000 x 28%
Equipment	45,000	45,000/90,000	=	50%	60,000 x 50%
Tools	19,800	19,800/90,000	=	22%	60,000 x 22%
Total	$90,000				

2.

Truck list price	$16,000
Discount	(900)
Dealer prep	350
	$15,450
8% sales tax	1,236
Painting	90
Total cost	$16,776

A—Truck	16,776	
A—Cash		16,776
A—Prepaid insurance	700	
A—Cash		700
A—Prepaid license	60	
A—Cash		60

3.

Year	STL	DDB
19X4	$7,000	$15,000
19X5	7,000	7,500
19X6	7,000	3,750
19X7	7,000	1,750
Totals	$28,000	$28,000

a. STL: (30,000 − 2,000)/4 years = 7,000/ year

b. DDB: 30,000 x (2 x 25%) = 15,000
(30,000 − 15,000) x 50% = 7,500
(30,000 − 22,500) x 50% = 3,750
(30,000 − 26,250) x 50% = 1,875 however this would exceed the total amount of depreciation allowed (28,000), so only 1,750 is taken.

4.

19X3: (50,000 − 5,000)/5 years = $9,000

19X4: $\dfrac{\text{(remaining book value − salvage value)}}{\text{Remaining useful life}}$

[(50,000 − 18,000) − 8,000]/5 years = $4,800

CHAPTER 9

LIABILITIES

CHAPTER OVERVIEW

This chapter introduces the liability side of the balance sheet. Liabilities are one source of funds available to a company for the acquisition of assets. A creditor lends funds to a firm in exchange for a promise that the loan will be repaid in the future.

An item is recognized as a liability in the accounts if it requires a transfer of assets or services at a future date; if the future transfer cannot be avoided; and if the transaction is the result of an event that has already taken place. Long-term liabilities are valued at the present value of their future cash payments. Short-term liabilities are valued at the sum of the undiscounted future cash payments.

Current liabilities are those that come due within the next twelve months or within the normal operating cycle of the business—whichever is longer. Examples of current liabilities include accounts payable, wages and other payroll obligations, short-term notes and interest payable, income taxes payable, warranty liabilities, unearned revenues, and the current portion of long-term debt.

Commitments are signed agreements under which a firm has contracted to perform certain actions in the future. Commitments are not recognized as liabilities until at least one of the parties to the agreement has performed its obligation under the contract. Contingent liabilities are potential liabilities. The status of a contingency is ultimately determined when one or more future events occur, or fail to occur. A contingent liability is recognized in the accounts if it is likely that an asset has been impaired or a liability incurred, and if the amount of the loss can be reasonably estimated.

Deferred taxes arise because a firm uses different accounting methods for financial reporting than for income tax reporting. Both the deferral method and the liability method for calculating deferred taxes are discussed. In the calculation of deferred taxes, the deferral method focuses on the income statement while the liability method focuses on the balance sheet. Currently, the deferral method is GAAP in Canada; however, the Accounting Standards Board of the CICA is considering whether the liability method should be required instead.

LEARNING OBJECTIVES

1. Understand the conceptual basis for the recognition and valuation of liabilities.
2. Be able to identify current liabilities.
3. Be familiar with the recognition and disclosure requirements for commitments.
4. Be familiar with the recognition and disclosure requirements for contingent liabilities.
5. Be able to calculate the amount of deferred taxes using the deferral method.
6. Be aware of how the liability method differs from the deferral method.
7. Be aware of the disclosure requirements for income taxes.

CHAPTER REVIEW

1. Understand the conceptual basis for the recognition and valuation of liabilities. (pp. 457–460)

A liability is recognized when it meets three general recognition criteria:

- there must be a responsibility to transfer assets or services at a future date;
- the obligation cannot be avoided; and
- the event giving rise to the obligation must have already occurred.

Applying these criteria can be difficult at times. For example, a liability probably will not be recognized if there is sufficient uncertainty about the amount of the obligation or the timing of the transfer. In addition, determining which specific event in a series of related events actually gave rise to an obligation can be difficult (for example, a lawsuit). There is also the question of whether the act of signing a contract, such as a purchase commitment, requires that a liability be recognized. GAAP specifies that if neither party to a contract has performed any of its obligations under the contract, no liability has been incurred.

GAAP requires that liabilities be recorded at the present value of the future cash payments. The interest rate to be used in the calculation depends on the nature of the liability and the creditworthiness of the firm.

Learning Tip

GAAP does not allow the interest rate to be changed after the initial present value calculation has been made and recorded. Exceptions to this rule are permitted only for troubled debt restructuring transactions and for pension obligations.

Short-term liabilities are valued at the sum of the undiscounted future payments to be made because the difference between that amount and the present value of the payments is usually immaterial.

2. Be able to identify current liabilities (pp. 460–466)

Current liabilities are those debts and other obligations that come due within the next twelve months or within the normal operating cycle of the business, whichever is longer. Accounts payable are incurred when a firm buys goods and services from its suppliers. The due date of accounts payable is generally a short time after the purchase (30–60 days) of the goods or services. The supplier may offer a cash discount for early payment or impose a penalty for late payment.

Wages and other payroll payables include accrued expenses for wages earned but not yet paid to employees as of the financial statement date. These accruals also include amounts withheld from employees for income taxes, employment insurance (EI), Canada Pension Plan (CPP), and other voluntary deductions. In addition, the other payroll payables include the employer's portion of items such as EI, CPP, and other insurance.

Short-term notes and interest payable represent the principal owed and the interest accrued on debt that comes due within the current liability period.

Income taxes payable represents the liability for provincial and federal income taxes owing on the taxable income of the firm. Corporations are required to make monthly instalments to Reveue Canada. The amount of the payments is based on the tax liability of the previous year. Any amount that is still owing after the actual tax payable is calculated at the end of the year and must be remitted within two months of the year end.

Most firms guarantee the quality of the products that they offer consumers. These guarantees are called product warranties. If the product does not perform as it is warranted to perform, the customer may return it and the firm must either repair the product or replace it. In accordance with the matching principle, the cost of repairing or replacing defective products must be recorded in the same period as the original sale was recorded. As a result, the firm must make an estimate of the amount of the liability it will incur over the life of the warranty. A firm is able to do so by analyzing its own historical data and making projections.

Unearned revenues are down payments or other amounts from customers that are received in advance of the seller having provided goods or services. This is a liability because the seller is obliged to either provide the goods or services, or return the money. As the firm provides the goods or services the applicable portion of the liability is recognized as revenue; that is, transferred from the liability account to the sales revenue account.

The current portion of long-term debt is the amount of the long-term obligations that will come due within the current liability period.

3. Be familiar with the recognition and disclosure requirements for commitments. (pp. 466–467)

Companies sometimes enter into contracts that commit them to some future transaction; for example, an agreement by a pop bottler to purchase a quantity of sugar over the next year. These agreements are called purchase commitments. GAAP does not require that a mutually unexecuted contract be recognized in the accounts but does require that the details of the contract be disclosed. A partially executed contract, where one party to the contract has performed all or a part of its obligation, is recognized as a liability.

Learning Tip

For an example of the disclosure of a commitment see Exhibit 9-2 on page 466 of the text.

4. Be familiar with the recognition and disclosure requirements for contingent liabilities (pp. 467–469)

A contingent liability, or contingent loss, is only a potential liability. Whether or not it represents a loss is something that will be determined in the future—when one or more events occur or fail to occur. Because of the uncertainty involved in, first, predicting whether the confirming event will occur in the future and, second, predicting the amount of any payment required, determining if a contingency should be recognized in the accounts requires the exercise of informed judgement. Under GAAP, a contingent liability should be recognized as a loss on the income statement and a liability on the balance sheet if the following criteria are met.

1. It is **likely** that a future event will confirm that the entity has incurred an obligation to transfer assets or provide services.
2. The amount of the loss can be reasonably estimated.

If neither of the criteria is met but the potential for loss is material, the contingency should be disclosed in the notes to the financial statements.

Learning Tip

For an example of note disclosure see Exhibit 6-5 on page 468 of the text.

5. Be able to calculate the amount of deferred taxes using the deferral method. (pp. 469–475)

Deferred taxes arise because corporations use different accounting methods for financial reporting than for tax reporting.

The focus of the deferral method is the income statement. Each year, income tax expense is calculated on the net income before taxes as shown on the income statement. Income tax payable is calculated on the taxable income reported on the income tax return. The difference between the income tax expense and the income tax payable is deferred tax. Although the amount of deferred tax can be proven independently, it is often referred to as a "plug" figure; that is, the amount required to balance the journal entry.

Learning Tip

The journal entry to record income taxes using the deferral method is as follows.

OE— Income tax expense
L—Income tax payable
L—Deferred income tax

One reason for the difference between income tax expense and income tax payable in any year is the effect of timing differences. These are due to differences between GAAP and the income tax laws and regulations. They arise because certain revenues and expenses may be reported as part of accounting income in one period but as a part of taxable income in another period. Timing differences reverse and tend to cancel out over time. For example, using CCA methods, and early in the life of an asset, a firm could recognize more amortization for income tax purposes than recognized using straight line amortization for accounting purposes. The difference between amortization and CCA will reverse in the latter half of the asset's life because, of course, the maximum amount of amortization or CCA that can be taken over the life of an asset is its original cost.

Learning Tip

For a numeric example see Exhibits 9-6 and 9-7 on pages 471 and 472 of the text.

Differences that do not reverse over time are called permanent differences. Under GAAP, permanent differences are ignored in the computation of deferred taxes.

6. Be aware of how the liability method differs from the deferral method. (p. 475)

The focus of the liability method is on the balance sheet. Under this method, the measure of the future tax liability (deferred taxes) is calculated by making a set of assumptions about future revenues and expenses and by using future income tax rates. The current tax liability is based on the taxable income and tax rates in the current period. Income tax expense is the amount derived after the current and deferred tax liabilities have been calculated so it is said to be the "plug" figure.

Currently, the deferral method is GAAP in Canada. The Accounting Standards Board of the CICA is, however, considering adoption of the liability method in the future.

7. Be aware of the disclosure requirements for income taxes. (p. 476)

A corporation must disclose the following information about its income taxes. First, the firm must separate income tax expense into its components; that is, the current and deferred portions. Foreign income taxes might also be a component of income tax expense. Second, the firm must disclose the items that caused the deferred tax amounts to arise. Finally, the firm must reconcile the total income tax expense reported to the amount that would have been reported using statutory rates. The difference is usually caused by tax credits and other items that cause the average rate to be different from the statutory rate.

Learning Tip

For an example see Exhibit 9-10 on page 476 of the text.

SELF STUDY

MATCHING

Match the key terms to the best explanation.

Key Terms

A. Commitments
B. Contingent liability
C. Contingent loss
D. Deferral method
E. Deferred taxes
F. Liability
G. Liability method
H. Mutually unexecuted contract
I. Partially executed contract
J. Permanent differences
K. Current liabilities
L. Present value of future cash flows
M. Warranty
N. Temporary differences
O. Unearned revenues

Explanations

1. __ A contract in which one or both of the parties has performed a portion of its part of the agreement.
2. __ Obligations which become due within one year.
3. __ Cash received from customers in advance of a seller providing any goods or services.
4. __ A duty to transfer assets or provide services at a definite time in the future.
5. __ A potential loss for a firm that depends on the occurrence of a future event.
6. __ Accounts used to reconcile the difference between tax expense and taxes payable.
7. __ Timing differences that arise because a firm uses different accounting methods for book and for tax purposes.
8. __ A method of calculating deferred taxes that is based on an estimate of future revenues, expenses, and tax rates.
9. __ Obligations a firm has agreed to perform but that do not yet meet the recognition criteria.
10. __ A method that computes the deferred tax amount as a plug figure needed to balance the difference between tax expense and taxes payable.
11. __ An explicit or implicit guarantee given by the seller of a product to the buyer.
12. __ Differences between book and tax reporting that never reverse themselves.
13. __ A contract in which neither party has performed its part of the agreement.
14. __ A potential liability of a firm that depends on some future event occurring.
15. __ The valuation of long-term debt.

ASSESS YOUR RECALL

1. Discuss the difference between a mutually unexecuted contract and a partially executed contract.

2. Define current liabilities and provide three examples of accounts that would be classified as such.

3. Explain the circumstances under which a contingent liability must be accrued or must simply be disclosed.

4. Explain the difference between the deferral method and the liability method of accounting for deferred taxes.

APPLYING YOUR KNOWLEDGE

1. The products sold by Belamy, Inc. carry a 3-year warranty against defects. Based on the company's experience, the estimated warranty costs as a percentage of sales are: 2% in the first year after a sale; 4% in the next year; and 8% in the third year. Sales and actual warranty costs for a recent 3-year period were:

Period	Sales	Actual Warranty Costs
19X1	$100,000	$ 2,250
19X2	137,000	6,800
19X3	162,000	19,500

a. Prepare the journal entries to record the estimated warranty expense and the actual warranty costs for each year.

b. Calculate the amount of the warranty payable shown on the balance sheet at the end of each year.

2. Becker, Inc. is the defendent in a lawsuit in which the plaintiff is suing for $250,000. For each of the following independent assumptions, indicate how this contingency should be handled. Provide the journal entry if one is required.

a. The company's lawyers believe it is likely that the company will be held liable but the amount cannot be reasonably estimated.
b. The company's lawyers believe it is not likely that the company will be held liable but they believe the amount of the claim is reasonable.
c. The company's lawyers believe it is likely that the company will be held liable and that the amount of the claim is reasonable.

3. Boyd, Inc. reported the following amounts (in thousands) for book and tax purposes for its first three years of operations.

	Year 1	Year 2	Year 3
Pretax book income	$150	$140	$220
Taxable income	120	160	170

The difference between book and taxable income are due to amortization/CCA differences. The income tax rate was 40% for all three years. Prepare the journal entry to record income tax expense for each year.

SOLUTIONS TO CHAPTER 9

MATCHING

1.	I	6.	E	11.	M
2.	K	7.	N	12.	J
3.	O	8.	G	13.	H
4.	F	9.	A	14.	B
5.	C	10.	D	15.	L

ASSESS YOUR RECALL

1. Mutually unexecuted contracts: Neither party to the contract has performed its part of the agreement. They are not recorded as they do not meet the recognition criteria.

Partially executed contracts: One party has performed a portion or all of its obligation under the contract. The activity performed is recorded; for example, if the buyer has made a payment for goods to be delivered, the seller would recognize the cash received as unearned revenue.

2. Current liabilities are those debts and obligations that come due within the next twelve months or normal operating cycle of the business, whichever is longer. Examples include: accounts payable, wages and payroll payables, short-term debt and interest payable, income tax payable, warranty payable, unearned revenue, and the current portion of long-term debt.

3. a. The contingency must be accrued as a liability when it is likely that a future event will confirm that an asset has been impaired or an obligation incurred and the amount can be reasonably estimated.

   b. The contingency must be disclosed but not accrued when the future event is likely to occur but the amount cannot be reasonably estimated.

   c. Neither accrual nor disclosure is required when it is unlikely that the future event will occur; however, note disclosure is allowed when the potential loss to the company is significant.

4. Deferral method: Focuses on the income statement. Calculates income tax expense and income taxes payable using the tax rates in effect for the current period. The difference between the two is the amount of deferred taxes (a plug figure).

Liability method: Focuses on the balance sheet. Determines the current tax liability using the current tax rates. Estimates the future tax liability (the deferred taxes) based on a set of assumptions about future revenues and expenses and uses the tax rates applicable in those future years. The difference between the current tax liability and the deferred tax liability is the tax expense (a plug figure).

APPLYING YOUR KNOWLEDGE

1. a.

	19X1		19X2		19X3	
SE-Warranty exp.	14,000		19,180		22,680	
L-Warranty pay		14,000		19,180		22,680
L-Warranty pay	2,250		6,800		19,500	
A-Cash		2,250		6,800		19,500

b.

19X1: 14,000 − 2,250 = $11,750

19X2: 11,750 + 19,180 − 6,800 = $24,130

19X3: 24,130 + 22,680 − 19,500 = $27,310

2. a. Since Becker is likely to lose the lawsuit but the amount cannot be estimated, it will be sufficient to disclose the contingent liability in the notes to the financial statements.

   b. Since the lawyers believe that it is unlikely that Becker will lose the lawsuit, neither accrual nor disclosure is required. The amount of $250,000 is said to be reasonable, however, and appears to be material. If this amount poses a significant risk to Becker, then it would be advisable to disclose the contingency in the notes to the financial statements.

   c. Since Becker is likely to lose the lawsuit and the amount can be estimated, it should be accrued. The journal entry is as follows.

SE—Loss Due to Lawsuit	250,000	
L—Estimated Liability on Lawsuit		250,000

3. Year 1

SE-Income tax expense ($150 x 40%)	60,000	
L-Income tax payable ($120 x 40%)		48,000
L-Deferred tax		12,000

Year 2

SE-Income tax expense ($140 x 40%)	56,000	
L-Deferred tax		8.000
L-Income tax payable ($160 x 40%)		64,000

Year 3

SE-Income tax expense ($220 x 40%)	88,000	
L-Income tax payable ($170 x 40%)		68,000
L-Deferred tax		20,000

CHAPTER 10

LONG-TERM LIABILITIES

CHAPTER OVERVIEW

The focus of this chapter is long-term liabilities. Bonds payable, lease liabilities, pensions, and other employment benefits are discussed.

Bonds are a means by which a firm can raise money for long-term requirements. Bonds have different forms and a variety of characteristics. A firm sells its bond issue to an investment banker or syndicate which in turn, sells the issue to its clients. A bond contains two promises: a promise to make semiannual interest payments on the face value of the bond and a promise to pay the face value of the bond at maturity. As a result, the selling price of a bond issue is equal to the present value of its interest payments plus the present value of its face value. The relationship between the coupon rate of the bond and the market, or discount, rate will determine if the bond sells at par, at a discount, or at a premium.

Leasing provides an alternative to the outright purchase of capital assets. From the point of view of a lessee, a lease can be classified as an operating lease, if it is a simple rental agreement, or as a capital lease, if it is in substance a purchase. A lease is considered to be a capital lease if it meets even one of the three capital lease criteria. If none of the criteria is met, the lease is considered to be an operating lease. Operating leases are treated like rental agreements. Capital leases are treated like the purchase of an asset and the acquisition of a related liability. Under a capital lease, the lessee recognizes both a leased asset and a lease liability equal in amount to the present value of the future lease payments. Since the substance of the transaction is a purchase, the lessee will recognize both the amortization of the asset and interest expense on the liability.

Pensions are contracts between an employer and employee that provide certain benefits to the employee upon retirement. There are two types of pension plans:

defined contribution plans and defined benefit plans. Under the first, the employer agrees to make a fixed contribution to the plan for each employee. Under the second, the employer agrees to pay the employee a certain amount during each year of retirement based upon a formula. Each year firms must accrue a pension expense amount. Many firms also provide other employment benefit plans such as health care and insurance.

LEARNING OBJECTIVES

1. Be familiar with the different types of bonds and their characteristics.
2. Be able to calculate the initial selling price of a bond.
3. Understand how bonds are reported in the financial press.
4. Be able to prepare the journal entries to record the issuance of a bond.
5. Be aware of the accounting issues related to the early retirement of debt and debt for equity swaps.
6. Understand the accounting and disclosure issues for a lessee.
7. Be familiar with the different types of pension plans.
8. Be aware of how long-term liabilities contribute to financial statement analysis.

CHAPTER REVIEW

1. Be aware of the different types of bonds and their characteristics. (pp. 493–495)

Bonds are a means by which a company can raise money for long-term requirements. A bond is an agreement between a borrower (the firm) and a lender (the investor) that outlines the conditions of the loan including how the borrower is to repay the lender.

The indenture agreement states the face value, maturity date, interest payment dates, and the coupon rate of the bond. All bond indentures require semiannual interest payments based on the face value of the bond and the coupon rate. An investment banker is usually engaged to assist the borrower in meeting the current demands of the market and in developing the most attractive bond issue for that market.

Some bonds require collateral and some do not. Mortgage bonds are secured by real property while collateral trust bonds are secured by the long-term investment portfolio of the firm. Debenture bonds, on the other hand, are secured solely by the creditworthiness of the issuer.

Bonds can contain special provisions that make them more attractive to investors. Convertible bonds, for example, allow bond holders to convert their bonds to common shares at some time in the future.

2. Be able to calculate the initial selling price of a bond. (pp. 498–501)

The price investors are willing to pay for a bond is equal to the present value of the cash flows they will receive from the bond. The formula is as follows.

Bond price = P.V. of coupon payments + P.V. of face value

The coupon payments are the semiannual interest payments which are based on the bond's face value and coupon rate. The equation is as follows.

Coupon payment = Face value x Coupon rate x 1/2

Tables of values used in making present value calculations are in the Appendix to the text (p. 707). Each table consists of factors which are derived using the discount rate and the length of time to maturity.

Learning Tip

Two pieces of information are needed to be able to use the tables: the number of periods of time and the interest rate. The number of periods of time is equal to the number of years to maturity multiplied by the number of interest payments per year. The interest rate is the market, or discount, rate divided by the number of interest payments per year.

If a bond sells for an amount equal to its face value, it is said to be issued at par. If the selling price exceeds the face value of the bond, it is said to be issued at a premium. Finally, if the selling price is less than the face value of the bond, the bond is said to be issued at a discount.

Learning Tip

The relationship between the coupon rate of a bond and the discount rate determines if a bond sells at par, at a premium, or at a discount.

If discount rate = coupon rate: bond sells at par
If discount rate < coupon rate: bond sells at a premium
If discount rate > coupon rate: bond sells at a discount

For a numeric example see Exhibit 10-4 on page 501 of the text.

3. Understand how bonds are reported in the financial press. (pp. 495–498)

The announcement of an initial bond issue (a tombstone ad) is published in the financial press—both newspapers and magazines. Information on issued bonds is quoted in the stock and bond section of daily newspapers. The data usually consists of the name of the issuing company, the coupon rate, the maturity date, the current yield, the number of bonds traded for the day, the closing price, and the net change in price from the previous day.

Learning Tip

For examples see Exhibits 10-1 and 10-2 on pages 496 and 497 of the text.

4. Be able to prepare the journal entries to record the issuance of a bond. (pp. 501–509)

Bonds sell at par when the cash proceeds equal the face value of the bond (discount rate = coupon rate). The journal entries to record the various events over the life of a bond sold at par are as follows.

At issue date		
A—Cash	XX	
L—Bonds Payable		XX
Interest accrual		
SE—Interest Expense	XX	
L—Interest Payable		XX
Interest payment		
L—Interest Payable	XX	
A—Cash		XX
At maturity date		
L—Bonds Payable	XX	
A—Cash		XX

Learning Tip

For a numeric examples see pages 501–501 and Exhibit 10-6 on page 504 of the text.

Bonds sell at a discount when the cash proceeds are less than the face value of the bond (the discount rate > the coupon rate). The difference between the cash proceeds and the face value is recorded in a contra-liability account called Discount on Bonds Payable. This amount represents an additional interest expense to the issuer because the firm must pay back more than it received. GAAP requires that the discount be amortized over the life of the bond. This has the effect of increasing the interest expense each interest payment period. The amount of amortization recognized each interest payment period is equal to the difference between the interest expense and the interest payable amounts. The interest formulas are as follows.

Interest expense = Principal x Discount rate x Time
Interest payable = Face value x Coupon rate x Time
Discount amortization = Interest expense − Interest payable

Learning Tip

In the above formula, the principal is the book value of the bond. Book value is equal to the Bonds Payable balance minus the Discount on Bonds Payable balance.

The journal entries to record the various events over the life of a bond sold at a discount are as follows:

At issue		
A—Cash	XX	
XL—Discount on Bonds Payable	XX	
L—Bonds Payable		XX
Interest accrual		
SE—Interest Expense	XX	
XL—Discount on Bonds Payable		XX
L—Interest Payable		XX
Interest payment		
L—Interest Payable	XX	
A—Cash		XX
At maturity date		
L—Bonds Payable	XX	
A—Cash		XX

Learning Tip

Over the life of the bond, as the discount is amortized, the book value of the bond increases until it equals the face value of the bond (maturity value).

For a numeric example see pages 504–506 of the text.

Bonds sell at a premium when the cash proceeds exceed the face value of the bond (discount rate < coupon rate). The difference between the cash proceeds and the face value is recorded in an adjunct account called Premium on Bonds Payable. This amount represents a reduction in the amount of interest expense recognized by the issuing firm because the firm will pay back less than it received. GAAP requires that the premium be amortized over the life of the bond. This has the effect of reducing the interest expense each interest payment period. The amount of amortization recognized each interest payment period is equal to the difference between the interest expense and the interest payable amounts. The interest expense and interest payable formulas are the same as those used for a bond sold at a discount. The premium amortization formula is as follows.

$$\text{Premium amortization} = \text{Interest payable} - \text{Interest expense}$$

Learning Tip

For bonds sold at a premium, principal is the book value of the bond. Book value is equal to the sum of the Bonds Payable and the Premium on Bonds Payable account balances.

The journal entries to record the various events over the life of a bond sold at a premium are:

At issuance		
A—Cash	XX	
L—Premium on Bonds Payable		XX
L—Bonds Payable		XX
Interest accrual		
SE—Interest Expense	XX	
L—Premium on Bonds Payable	XX	
L—Interest Payable		XX
Interest payment		
L—Interest Payable	XX	
A—Cash		XX
At maturity date		
L—Bonds Payable	XX	
A—Cash		XX

Learning Tip

Over the life of a bond, as the premium is amortized, the book value of the bond decreases until it equals the face value of the bond (at maturity).

For numeric examples see pages 506–509 and Exhibits 10-9 and 10-10 on pages 508 and 509 of the text.

5. Be aware of the accounting issues related to the early retirement of debt and debt for equity swaps. (pp. 509–510)

If bonds are retired before they mature any gain or loss on the transaction must be reported on the income statement.

Learning Tip

For an example of the journal entry to record an early retirement with a gain, see the box on page 509 of the text.

When bonds are exchanged for shares of common stock, in what is called a debt for equity swap, the firm must transfer the carrying value of the bonds being exchanged into the capital accounts. There is no gain or loss recognized on the exchange.

Learning Tip

For an example of the journal entry see the box on page 510 of the text.

6. Understand the accounting and disclosure issues for a lessee. (pp. 510–515)

A firm that leases, or rents, an asset from another firm is called the lessee. A lease contract may be classified as either an operating lease or a capital lease. If the lease contract meets even one of the following criteria it must be classified as a capital lease.

1. Title to the asset passes to the lessee at the end of the lease term or the lease contains a bargain purchase option.
2. The lease term is equal to at least 75% of the useful life of the asset.

3. The present value of the minimum lease payments is at least 90% of the fair market value of the asset.

If none of the above criteria is met, the lease must be classified as an operating lease. For an operating lease, the only journal entry required to record the periodic lease payment is as follows:

OE—Lease (Rent) Expense	XX	
A—Cash		XX

A capital lease must be recorded as if it were the outright purchase of an asset and the assumption of a corresponding liability. The asset and the liability are recorded at an amount equal to the present value of the lease payments. The initial journal entry is as follows.

A—Leased Asset	XX	
L—Lease Liability		XX

Learning Tip

For a numeric example see the second box on page 513 of the text.

Lease payments are usually made at the beginning of each period. They are, therefore, treated as an annuity in advance. For an example of the calculation of the present value of a capital lease, see the box at the bottom of page 512 of the text.

Because a capital lease is considered to be equivalent to the purchase of an asset and the assumption of debt, the lessee will record both amortization expense on the asset and interest expense on the liability. The journal entries take the following form:

SE—Amortization Expense	XX	
XA—Accumulated Amortization		XX
SE—Interest Expense	XX	
L—Lease Liability		XX

Lease payments reduce the liability account:

L—Lease liability	XX	
A—Cash		XX

Learning Tip

Over the life of a lease the total of the expenses recognized by the lessee and the total cash outflow will be the same regardless of whether the lease is accounted for as a capital lease or an operating lease. The only difference between the two methods is the timing of the expense recognition.

Whether a lease is accounted for as an operating lease or a capital lease, GAAP requires that both the total of the future payments on the lease as well as the payments due in each of the next five years be disclosed in the notes to the financial statements. For capital leases GAAP also requires that the nature of the leased assets and the terms of the liability be disclosed in the notes.

7. Be familiar with the different types of pension plans. (pp. 516–518)

Pensions are agreements between a firm and its employees that provide certain benefits to the employees upon retirement. There are two kinds of pension plans—defined contribution plans and defined benefit plans.

In a defined contribution plan the employer makes a contribution (usually a percentage of an employee's salary) to a retirement fund for each employee. Employees may also make their own contributions to the plan in order to increase the amount invested on their behalf. The firm makes its contributions to a pension fund which is managed by a trustee. The assets of the fund are not part of the assets of the firm. The amount of the payments to retirees depends on how well the pension fund has performed over time.

Learning Tip

For an example of the journal entries to accrue the expense and satisfy the liability, see the box on page 516 of the text.

In a defined benefit plan, the employer guarantees to pay its employees a certain amount during each year of retirement. The amount of the payment is based on a formula which includes factors such as the employee's length of service and salary (usually an average of the highest three years). The pension obligation is calculated as the present value of the future pension plan outflows. The calculation is usually made by an actuary engaged by the company.

Most pension plan agreements require the corporation to fund the pension plan; that is, to remit regular cash payments to the trustee for the fund. Note however, that the amount of a contribution to the fund does not have to equal the amount of the annual pension expense. As a result, the fair value of the assets in the fund and the amount of the pension obligation may not be the same. If they are the same, the fund is said to be fully funded. If the fair value of the assets in the fund is greater than the liability, the fund is said to be overfunded. Finally, if the fair value of the assets in the fund is less than the liability, the fund is said to be underfunded.

8. Be aware of how long-term liabilities contribute to financial statement analysis. (pp. 518–523)

When analyzing the financial statements of a company the following questions about long-term liabilities should be considered.

- Whether there are any unrecorded liabilities such as operating leases or postretirement employment benefits.
- Whether the book values of the liabilities reflect relatively current interest rates.
- Whether there have been significant fluctuations in the exchange rate for debt that must be repaid in a foreign currency.
- Whether the company has incurred a significant amount of debt agreements with variable-rate interest provisions.

Two ratios which are useful in evaluating the ability of the company to meet its obligations as they come due are the **debt/equity ratio** and the **times interest earned ratio**.

$$\text{Debt/equity ratio} = \frac{\text{Total liabilities}}{\text{Total liabilities} + \text{Shareholders' equity}}$$

The debt/equity ratio shows how much of a firms assets are financed by debt. Lenders and investors will want to see a reasonable balance between the extent to which assets are financed by debt or by equity investment.

$$\text{Times interest earned} = \frac{\text{Net income} + \text{Taxes} + \text{Interest}}{\text{Interest}}$$

This ratio is a measure of the ability of the company to meet its interest obligations out of current earnings. Clearly, if earnings are insufficient to cover interest expense, the company will soon be in a deficit position.

As with all ratio analysis, it is important to consider the ratios for a company over time in order to determine if there are any trends in evidence.

SELF STUDY

MATCHING

Match the key term to the best explanation.

Key Terms

A. Actuary
B. Bond covenants
C. Capital lease
D. Defined benefit plan
E. Defined contribution plan
F. Discount
G. Indenture agreement
H. Lessee
I. Lessor
J. Maturity date
K. Operating lease
L. Overfunded
M. Debt/equity ratio
N. Underwriter
O. Vesting

Explanations

1. __An investment bank that arranges and sells the initial bond issue for a company.
2. __When a firm must repay the face value of a bond.
3. __When pension plan assets exceed the pension obligation.
4. __When the cash proceeds from the sale of a bond are less than its face value.
5. __The professional who is engaged to calculate the present value of the pension obligation.
6. __A lease for which the present value of the lease payments is recorded by the lessee as an asset and a related liability.
7. __The firm that is making lease payments for the use of an asset.
8. __Total liabilities/Total liabilities + Shareholders' equity.
9. __Restrictions placed on a firm that issues bonds.
10. __A provision that guarantees that employees will receive their pension benefits, even if they leave the employ of the firm.
11. __A pension plan that specifies the amount that a firm must contribute to the fund for its employees.
12. __Specifies the terms and restrictions connected with the issuance of a bond.
13. __The party receiving the lease payments.
14. __A lease in which the lessee expenses the lease payments.
15. __A pension plan that specifies the benefits that employees will receive upon retirement.

ASSESS YOUR RECALL

1. Describe the basic characteristics of a bond and indicate how bonds differ from share capital.

2. Explain the difference between the par value and the selling price of a bond. When are they the same? Different?

3. Describe a debt for equity swap.

4. Briefly describe an operating lease and a capital lease from the point of view of the lessee.

5. Which type of lease will be the most expensive for the lessee? Identify the expenses recognized under each type of lease.

6. Identify the three parties involved in the accounting for and the reporting of the pension plan of a company.

APPLYING YOUR KNOWLEDGE

1. Bandini Corporation issued 300 five-year, 8% bonds to yield 10%. (Recall that bonds are usually issued in $1,000 denominations.)

   a. Compute and record the issue price.
   b. Compute and record the interest expense and the interest payments for the first year.
   c. Compute the book value (principal) at the beginning of the second year.

a) Issued 300 bonds × $1000 = $300,000
t = 5year
8% bonds to 10% yield

Issuance price

Cash
Discount on Bonds Payable
Bonds payable 300,000

PV = Int pmt. + PV of FV
=

2. On January 1, 19X4, Mercy Co. Ltd. leased a piece of equipment from Windsor Manufacturing that cost $240,000 to produce. The lease term and the useful life of the equipment are both 5 years. The equipment has no residual value. The contract calls for annual payments of $80,409 in advance on January 1 of each year and a 15% interest rate. Mercy Co. Ltd. uses straight-line amortization for its assets and closes its books on December 31.

a. How should Mercy account for this lease? Why?
b. Prepare the 19X4 journal entries required for this lease on the books of Mercy.

SOLUTIONS TO CHAPTER 10

MATCHING

1. N	6. C	11. E
2. J	7. H	12. G
3. L	8. M	13. I
4. F	9. B	14. K
5. A	10. O	15. D

ASSESS YOUR RECALL

1. Bonds are formal agreements under which the borrower agrees to pay the bondholder (investor) periodic interest and to return the face value of the bond at the maturity date. Each bond consists of a coupon interest rate, a face value, and a maturity date.

Bonds differ from share capital in that they do not represent an ownership interest. They have no voting rights and do not receive dividends. Bondholders receive interest payments semiannually as specified by the terms of the bond. Shareholders receive dividends only when and if the firm decides to declare them. The bondholders are repaid the face value of the bond at maturity but the face value of a share is not usually repaid.

2. The par value of a bond is its face value. The issue price of the bond is the amount that the bond sells for to investors in the market. They are the same when the issue price equals the par value; that is, the bond sells at par. They are different when the bond sells at a discount or premium.

3. In a debt for equity swap, the holder of a convertible bond exercises the option to convert the bond into common shares. At the time of conversion, the carrying value of the bonds is removed from the bond accounts and transferred to the common share accounts. Gains or losses are not recognized on swaps.

4. An operating lease is a simple rental agreement in which the lessee pays a rental fee to the lessor for the use of the asset. At the end of the lease term, the asset is returned to the lessor.

A capital lease is considered to be the same as the purchase of an asset and the assumption of a corresponding liability. The lessee has all the risks and rewards of ownership. A capital lease is recorded as if it were a purchase.

5. The total expense to the lessee is the same regardless of whether the lease is accounted for as an operating lease or a capital lease. The only difference between the two methods is in the timing of the expense recognition. In an operating lease the expense consists solely of the lease payments (usually spread evenly over the

lease term). In a capital lease the expenses consist of amortization expense and interest expense.

6. The three parties are the employer, the trustee, and the actuary.

APPLYING YOUR KNOWLEDGE

1. a.

Issue price

Present value = P.V. of coupon pymts. + P.V. of maturity pmt of the bond
= (12,000 x 7.72173) + (300,000 x 0.61391)
= 276,834

Journal entry

A—Cash	276,834	
XL—Discount on Bonds Payable	23,166	
L—Bonds Payable		300,000

b.

Interest expense = Principal x Discount rate x Time
First 6-months

= 276,834 x 10% x 6/12
= 13,842

Interest payable = Face amount x Coupon rate x Time
First 6-months

= 300,000 x 8% x 6/12
= 12,000

Journal entries

OE—Interest Expense	13,842	
XL—Discount on Bonds Payable		1,842
L—Interest Payable		12,000
L—Interest Payable	12,000	
A—Cash		12,000

Interest payable = (276,834 + 1,842) x 10% x 6/12
Second 6-months

= 13,934

Interest payable = 300,000 x 8% x 6/12
Second 6-months

= 12,000

Journal entries

OE—Interest Expense	13, 934	
XL—Discount on Bonds Payable		1, 934
L—Interest Payable		12,000
L—Interest Payable	12,000	
A—Cash		12,000

c.

Principal = Beginning book value + discount amortization
= (300,000 − 23,166) + 1,842 + 1,934
= 280,610

2\. a. Mercy is the lessee and should account for this lease as a capital lease because the lease term is at least 75% of the asset's useful life. In this case it is 100%.

b.

Lessee journal entries (Mercy Co.)

1/ 1/X4:	A—Leased Equipment	309,975	
	L—Lease Obligation		229,566
	A—Cash		80,409
	*80,409 x 3.85498 = 309,975		
12/31/X4:	OE—Interest Expense	34,435	
	L—Lease Obligation		34,435
	*229,566 x 15% = 34,435		
	OE—Amortization Expense	61,995	
	XA—Accumulated Amortization		61,995
	*309,975/5 years = 61,995		

CHAPTER 11

SHAREHOLDERS' EQUITY

CHAPTER OVERVIEW

This chapter concludes coverage of the balance sheet with a discussion of the elements of shareholders' equity. The chapter begins with a discussion of the different forms of business organization (sole proprietorship, partnership, and corporation) and points out the advantages and disadvantages of each.

Corporations are formed under either federal or provincial statute. Regardless of the jurisdiction of incorporation, the organizers of the company must file articles of incorporation which will specify the kind of shares the corporation can issue. In general, the shares issued by corporations fall into two categories—common shares and preferred shares. Common shareholders enjoy a set of rights that are not all shared by the preferred shareholders. On the other hand, preferred shareholders enjoy certain preferences that compensate for the loss of any rights.

It is becoming rare in Canada for a corporation to issue shares having a par value. The concept of par value has rather murky history and the reasons for requiring par value no longer apply. However, in those rare cases that par value shares exist and the issue price is greater than the par value, the excess amount is credited to Contributed Capital. Treasury shares, that is shares that the issuing corporation repurchases in the market and holds for subsequent reissue, are also becoming a rarity in Canada. The concept of treasury shares has historical roots. Earlier corporations' acts required that incorporators specify the number of shares the corporation was authorized to issue. Since most of the current statutes have done away with authorized capital, the issue of how to account for treasury shares is disappearing. Most jurisdictions require that repurchased shares be retired. Treasury share costs are debited to a contra-equity account called treasury shares. When treasury shares are reissued, any difference between the reissue price and the purchase cost is recorded in contributed capital or retained earnings.

Dividends are declared at the discretion of the board of directors. Dividends may be paid in cash, in kind (other property), or in additional shares. Property dividends are recognized at the fair market value of the property given up. Small stock dividends (less than 20%) are recognized at the fair market value of the shares while large stock dividends (more than 25%) are recognized at the carrying value of the shares.

The chapter concludes with a discussion of stock splits and employee stock option plans.

LEARNING OBJECTIVES

1. Be familiar with the advantages and disadvantages of the different forms of business organization.
2. Be familiar with the characteristics of common shares and preferred shares.
3. Be able to account for the issue of common shares and for treasury share transactions.
4. Be able to account for cash and property dividends.
5. Be aware of the accounting issues related to stock dividends, stock splits, and employee stock options.
6. Be aware of how shareholders' equity contributes to financial statement analysis.

CHAPTER REVIEW

1. Be familiar with the advantages and disadvantages of the different forms of business organization. (pp. 545–548)

A business may be formed as a sole proprietorship, a partnership, or a corporation. A sole proprietorship has a single owner who makes all the business decisions and has complete control of the company. A sole proprietorship is the easiest form of business to establish. There are relatively few legal requirements involved and, therefore, a minimum of paperwork. A proprietorship is not a legal entity that is separate from its owner. This means that the owner and the business are considered to be one and the same. As a result, the profits from the business are taxed as personal income to the owner. The company does not file a tax return and does not report income tax expense on its income statement. In addition, the owner has personal responsibility (unlimited liability) for the debts of the business.

A partnership is similar to a sole proprietorship except for the fact that there is more than one owner of the business. The owners, or partners, also have unlimited liability for the debts of the firm. A limited partnership is slightly different from a general partnership in that it has some of the characteristics of a corporation. In a limited partnership, only the general partners have unlimited liability. The limited partners have only the amount of their investment at risk; that is, they enjoy limited liability. The general partners usually run the business and make all decisions; the limited partners are often referred to as "silent" partners.

A corporation is a separate legal entity. A corporation can enter into contracts, is obliged to file a tax return, and can sue and be sued—it is completely separate from its owners. The shareholders of a corporation have limited liability; however, except in closely held corporations, they lose a degree of control over the entity because business decisions are made by a board of directors which also hires the officers and managers of the company. The shareholders have some control over the business in that they can elect the members of the board of directors. Finally, there is a significant amount of paperwork and regulation involved in forming and maintaining a corporation.

Corporations are formed under federal or provincial corporations acts; for example, the Canada Business Corporations Act governs corporations formed under federal statute. An application to incorporate a business entity must include a document called the articles of incorporation. The articles specify the type of business that will be conducted, how the Board of Directors will be organized, who the management will be, and a description of the shares that will be issued.

2. Be familiar with the characteristics of common shares and preferred shares. (pp. 548–555)

There are two general types of shares issued by a corporation: common shares and preferred shares. Each of these types of shares may be further subdivided into classes; for example, Class A and Class B Common Shares. Each classification and/or subdivision of share has characteristics which distinguish it from the other classifications.

Common shares carry with them a set of rights, based on percentage of ownership, that allows the owners to share proportionately in profits and losses, the selection of management, the assets upon liquidation, and subsequent issues of shares. This latter right is called a preemptive right—it may or may not be provided depending on the jurisdiction of incorporation.

A holder of preferred shares gives up the right to vote in exchange for certain privileges. Although the privileges can vary among different issues of preferred shares, some typical privileges include the right to receive dividends at a certain rate which must be paid before dividends can be paid to the common shareholders and a preferential claim on the assets of the corporation. Preferred shares may also be designated as **participating**, **cumulative**, **convertible**, **redeemable**, or **rectractable**. If a preferred share is participating, the preferred shareholders will share in any excess dividends declared for the common shareholders; if cumulative, dividends in arrears must be paid to the preferred shareholders before current dividends can be paid to the common shareholders. If they are convertible, they may be converted to common shares; if redeemable, they can be sold back to the corporation; if retractable, the shares can be bought back by the corporation. All of the latter provisions are subject to certain conditions having been met.

3. Be able to account for the issue of common shares and for treasury share transactions. (pp. 555–557)

To record the issue of common shares, a corporation will debit the cash account and credit a common shares account. In some jurisdictions, shares may be issued with a par, or stated, value. The designation "par value" has long since lost any significance; as a result, most corporations acts in Canada specify that shares will be issued without par value. In the event, however, that existing par value shares are issued for an amount that is greater than par value, the excess should be credited to the contributed capital account. The journal entries to record the issue of shares are as follows:

Par value common shares		
A—Cash	XX	
SE—Common shares		XX
SE—Contributed capital		XX
Shares without par value		
A—Cash	XX	
SE—Common Shares		XX

A firm will occassionally buy back its own shares either because it wants to reduce the number of shares outstanding or because it needs shares to satisfy stock option plans. Such repurchased shares, if not retired, are called treasury shares. They are recorded in a contra-equity account called Treasury Shares. Treasury shares are shown on the balance sheet as a reduction of the other shareholders' equity accounts.

The purchase of treasury shares is recorded at cost. The reissue of the shares is recorded at the selling price of the shares. If the selling price of the treasury shares exceeds the cost, the excess is credited to the Contributed Capital account. If the selling price is less than the cost, the difference is debited to the Contributed Capital account to the extent that the account has a balance. If Contributed Capital is exhausted the remainder is debited to the Retained Earnings account. The journal entries to record a purchase, a sale at a price above cost, and a sale at a price below cost are illustrated below.

Purchase		
XSE—Treasury shares	XX	
A—Cash		XX
Reissue above cost		
A—Cash	XX	
XSE—Treasury shares		XX
SE—Contributed capital		XX
Reissue below cost		
A—Cash	XX	
SE—Contributed capital	XX	
XSE—Treasury shares		XX

4. Be able to account for cash and property dividends. (pp. 557–559)

Dividends are declared by the board of directors at their discretion. There are three dates that are important in the accounting for dividends. The date of declaration is the date on which the dividend becomes a legal liability of the firm and the date on which the dividend must be recorded in the accounts. The date of record is the date on which the shareholders who are entitled to receive the dividend are identified. There are no journal entries associated with the date of record. The date of payment is the date on which the firm issues cheques to the shareholders in payment of the dividend.

Learning Tip

The ex-dividend day is the day after the date of record.

The journal entries on the date of declaration and date of payment are illustrated below.

Declaration date		
SE—Dividends declared	XX	
L—Dividends payable		XX
Payment date		
L—Dividends payable	XX	
A—Cash		XX

Learning Tip

The dividends declared account is closed to the retained earnings account at year end.

For a numeric example see the boxes on pages 557 and 558 of the text.

Under GAAP, property dividends are recognized at the fair market value of the asset being distributed. Any difference between the book value of the asset and its fair market value is recorded as a gain or a loss on the date of payment. The journal entries for the declaration and payment of a property dividend (illustrating first a gain and then a loss) are as follows:

Declaration		
SE—Property dividend declared	XX	
L—Dividend payable		XX
Payment with a gain		
L—Dividend payable	XX	
A—Asset (at cost)		XX
SE—Gain on asset		XX
Payment with a loss		
L—Dividend payable	XX	
SE—Loss on asset	XX	
A—Asset (at cost)		XX

Learning Tip

For a numeric example see the box on page 559 of the text.

5. Be aware of the accounting issues related to stock dividends, stock splits, and employee stock options. (pp. 559–561)

If a company declares a stock dividend, it intends to pay its shareholders a dividend in the form of additional shares in the company rather than cash or property. If the stock dividend declared is for a relatively small percentage of the total of issued capital it is referred to as a small stock dividend.

Small dividends are valued at the fair market value of the shares on the date of declaration. However, since the directors may revoke a stock dividend at any time before it is paid, the dividend is often not recorded until the payment date. If the dividend is recorded at the date of declaration, the credit is posted to Stock Dividends Issuable rather than Dividends Payable. Journal entries to record the dividend on the declaration are illustrated below.

Declaration date		
SE—Dividends declared	XX	
SE—Stock dividends issuable		XX
Payment date		
SE—Stock dividends issuable	XX	
SE—Common Shares		XX

Learning Tip

For a numeric example see the illustration on page 560 of the text.

Stock splits are usually declared with the intention of reducing the market price per share. There are no changes to the balances in the shareholders' equity accounts upon the declaration of a stock split. The only change is to the number of shares outstanding. As a result, it is sufficient to record a stock split by a memorandum entry.

Learning Tip

In a 3 for 1 split, because there would be three times as many new shares outstanding as old, the stock market would adjust the market price per share proportionately.

Employee stock option plans are usually granted as part of an incentive compensation plan. The plan allows employees to buy shares of the company at a fixed price (the exercise price) that is above the current market price at the time the option is granted. Presumably the employees will be motivated to work hard and thereby improve the profitability of the company so that the market price of the company's shares will rise above the exercise price of the option before it expires.

Under GAAP no entry is made at the date of the grant unless the exercise price is below the current market price. In any event, when the options are exercised and the stock is purchased, the transaction is recorded like any sale of shares.

Learning Tip

For an example of the disclosure of employee stock options see Exhibit 11-3 on page 562 of the text.

6. Be aware of how shareholders' equity contributes to financial statement analysis. (pp. 563–564)

Three important ratios using information about shareholders' equity are **earnings per share**, the **price/earnings ratio**, and **return on shareholders' equity**. The earnings per share ratio, which has been discussed in earlier chapters, relates the net income of the company to individual shares. The price/earnings ratio relates the market price per share to the earnings per share. It is calculated as follows.

Price/earnings ratio = Market price per share/Earnings per share

The return on shareholders' equity (ROE) relates net income available to common shareholders to total common shareholders' equity. It is calculated as follows.

$$\text{ROE} = \frac{\text{Net income} - \text{Preferred dividends}}{\text{Average common shareholders' equity}}$$

SELF STUDY

MATCHING

Match the key term to the best explanation

Key Terms

A. Articles of incorporation
B. Authorized shares
C. Date of declaration
D. Date of record
E. Dividends in arrears
F. General partners
G. Memorandum entry
H. Outstanding shares
I. Par value
J. Preemptive right
K. Prospectus
L. Corporation
M. Treasury shares
N. Unlimited liability
O. Employee stock options

Explanations

1. __ The date on which shares must be owned in order to receive a declared dividend.
2. __ A document which outlines the features of new share issues.
3. __ Issued shares minus treasury shares.
4. __ A characteristic of some forms of business organization that holds the owners responsible for the liabilities of the firm.
5. __ A separate legal entity whose owners are protected by unlimited liability.
6. __ The maximum number of shares that a corporation may issue under its charter.
7. __ A shareholder's right to share proportionately in any new issuances of common shares.
8. __ An entry made to record a stock split.
9. __ A document filed to conform to the requirements of the CBCA or the provincial corporations acts.
10. __ Often a feature of employee compensation plans.
11. __ A value per share of common stock set in the articles of incorporation in some jurisdictions.
12. __ Unpaid dividends on cumulative preferred shares.
13. __ Issued shares that are repurchased by the issuing company.
14. __ The date that a dividend becomes a legal liability.
15. __ Partners who have unlimited liability in a limited partnership.

ASSESS YOUR RECALL

1. Discuss the advantages and disadvantages of sole proprietorships, partnerships, and corporations.

2. Can one or more of the basic shareholder rights be withheld from shareholders? If so, explain how.

3. Describe the effects that purchases and subsequent sales of treasury shares have on a firm's assets, liabilities, and shareholders' equity.

4. Explain the difference between a property dividend and a stock dividend.

5. Compare and contrast stock dividends and stock splits.

APPLYING YOUR KNOWLEDGE

1. On December 31, 19X4, the shareholders' equity in Tallet Co. Ltd. was as follows.

Class A Common shares	\$400,000
Class B Common shares	125,000
Retained earnings	50,000
Total shareholders' equity	\$575,000

Prepare the journal entries for the following transactions that occurred during 19X5.

a. Sold 5,000 shares of the Class A common shares for \$12 a share.
b. Sold 10,000 shares of the Class B common shares for \$8 a share.
c. Repurchased 4,000 shares of the Class A common shares for \$14 a share.
d. Reissued 1,000 shares of the treasury shares for \$13 a share.
e. Reissued the remaining 3,000 shares of the treasury shares for \$9 a share.

2. Assume that a firm has 60,000 shares of $20 par value common shares and 5,000 shares of 5%, $100 par value preferred shares outstanding. No dividends have been declared in the previous two years.

a. Calculate the amount of the current dividend payable to each class of shares under each of the following independent assumptions.

Case 1:	Total dividend $50,000. Preferred shares are non-cumulative and nonparticipating.
Case 2:	Total dividend is $80,000. Preferred shares are cumulative and nonparticipating.
Case 3:	An 8% dividend is declared on the common shares. The preferred shares are cumulative and participating.

b. Assume that the dividend in Case 3 was declared on January 15, 19X4 for shareholders of record on January 29 and payable on February 6. Prepare the journal entries to record the dividend.

3. Yardley, Inc. has the following shareholders' equity accounts:

Common Shares, 40,000 shares issued and outstanding	$700,000
Retained earnings	1,750,000
Total shareholders' equity	$2,450,000

Prepare the journal entries for the following independent situations.

a. Declared a property dividend on February 2 for shareholders of record on February 15, and payable on March 3. The dividend consists of 20,000 shares in another company that Yardley is holding as a temporary investment (cost $30,000). The fair market value of the shares is $1.60 a share.

b. Declared a 10% stock dividend on March 1 for shareholders of record on March 15 and payable on March 30. The market price of Yardley's shares is $18.00 a share on the date of declaration.

c. Declared a 3 for 1 stock split.

d. What is the effect of situation "c" on shareholders' equity.

SOLUTIONS TO CHAPTER 11

MATCHING

1. D	6. B	11. I
2. K	7. J	12. E
3. H	8. G	13. M
4. N	9. A	14. C
5. L	10. O	15. F

ASSESS YOUR RECALL

1.

Sole proprietorship:

Advantages:	easy to form, retain control, the business itself is not taxed, limited paperwork and regulation
Disadvantages:	Unlimited liability, could be difficult to raise additional capital, profits taxed in the hands of the owner

Partnership:

Advantages:	same as sole proprietorships
Disadvantages:	same as sole proprietorships, control shared with other partners, requires a detailed partnership agreement to avoid problems

Corporation:

Advantages:	limited liability, ability to raise additional capital, taxed separately from owners
Disadvantages:	loss of control, excessive paperwork and regulation, double taxation.

2. If more than one class of common shares is issued, each class is differentiated by some amendment to the basic rights. In addition, preferred shares typically do not carry the right to vote.

3. The purchase of treasury shares reduces both assets (cash) and total shareholders' equity (the treasury shares account is a contra-equity account).

The sale of treasury stock increase both assets (cash) and total shareholders' equity (through reductions in the treasury share account at cost, and increases in contributed capital).

4. A property dividend is valued at the fair market value of the property distributed and results in the reduction of a firm's assets (the property) and shareholders' equity (retained earnings).

A stock dividend is valued at the fair market value of the additional shares issued. The result of the dividend is a reduction of retained earnings offset by an equal increase in the common shares account. There is no change in the firm's total assets or shareholders' equity.

5. Both stock dividends and stock splits leave the total of shareholders' equity unchanged, increase the number of shares issued and outstanding, and are declared to satisfy shareholders' demands for a return on their investment.

Stock dividends change the amounts of the elements within shareholders' equity. The amount of the dividend reduces retained earnings and increases common shares. Stock splits do not.

Stock splits increase the number of shares outstanding.

APPLYING YOUR KNOWLEDGE

1. a.

A—Cash	60,000	
SE—Class A common		60,000

b.

A—Cash	80,000	
SE- Class B common		80,000

c.

XSE—Treasury shares	56,000	
A—Cash		56,000

d.

A—Cash	13,000	
SE—Retained earnings	1,000	
XSE—Treasury shares		14,000

e.

A—Cash	27,000	
SE—Retained earnings	15,000	
XSE—Treasury shares		42,000

2.

a. Case 1:	Preferred dividend = 5% x $100 x 5,000	=	$25,000
	Common dividend = $50,000 − 25,000	=	$25,000
Case 2:	Dividends in arrears = $25,000 x 2	=	$50,000
	Current dividend	=	25,000
	Total preferred dividend	=	$75,000
	Common dividend = $80,000 − 75,000	=	$ 5,000

Case 3:	Dividends in arrears	= $50,000
	Current dividend	= 25,000
	Participating dividend:	
	(3% x $100 x 5,000)	= 15,000
	Total preferred dividend	= $90,000
	Common dividend = 8% x $20 x 60,000	= $96,000

b. 1/15/X4	OE—Dividends Declared	186,000	
	L—Dividends Payable		186,000
2/6/X4	L—Dividends Payable	186,000	
	A—Cash		186,000

3.

a. 2/1	SE—Property Dividend Declared	32,000	
	L—Dividends Payable		32,000
3/3	L—Dividends Payable	32,000	
	A—Temporary Investments		30,000
	SE—Gain on Temporary Inv.		2,000
b. 3/ 1	SE—Dividend Declared	72,000	
	SE—Stock Dividend Issuable		72,000
3/30	SE—Stock Dividend Issuable	72,000	
	SE—Common Shares		72,000

c. Memorandum entry that there are now 120,000 (40,000 x 3) shares issued and outstanding.

e. The stock split results in 40,000 shares being replaced with 120,000 shares. There is no change in the total of shareholders' equity or in the individual amounts.

CHAPTER 12

FINANCIAL STATEMENT ANALYSIS

CHAPTER OVERVIEW

This chapter takes a general approach to financial statement analysis and continues the discussion begun in the first eleven chapters. The chapter begins with a reminder that financial statements are used by different users for different purposes. Regardless of specific purpose, however, all users perform financial statement analysis in order to help them in decision making. Recall that, in order for information to be useful for decision making, it must be relevant. Information will be relevant if it has feedback value and predictive value. Financial statement analysis tools and techniques provide the means by which the users can assess past performance and predict future performance.

The chapter outlines the three types of data that are used in financial statement analysis: raw financial data, common size data, and ratio data. This data can be used to assess performance within a firm over time (time-series analysis) and/or across firms in the same industry (cross-sectional analysis). Raw financial data is the information that appears on the financial statements;for example, total assets or current liabilities. Common size data is derived by expressing each line item on the financial statements as a percentage of a common base; for example, expressing all items on the income statement as a percentage of sales. Ratio data expresses the relationship between two or more elements of data in the financial statements.

The ratios discussed in the chapter fall into three categories:

- performance ratios;
- short-term liquidity ratios; and
- long-term liquidity ratios.

The discussion focuses on both the calculation of the ratios and the interpretation of the results. The chapter also continues the discussion of earnings per share and the price/earnings ratio.

LEARNING OBJECTIVES

1. Understand the process involved in performing financial statement analysis.
2. Understand the connection between prospective analysis and retrospective analysis.
3. Be familiar with the types of data that are used in time-series analysis and cross-sectional analysis.
4. Be able to calculate and interpret the performance ratios.
5. Be able to calculate and interpret the turnover ratios.
6. Be able to calculate and interpret the short-term liquidity ratios.
7. Be able to calculate and interpret the long-term liquidity ratios.
8. Be familiar with the earnings per share and price/earnings ratios.

CHAPTER REVIEW

1. Understand the process involved in performing financial statement analysis. (pp. 591–593)

Financial statements are analyzed by different users for different purposes. The specific purpose will depend on the needs of the particular user. In general, however, the analysis is performed to help the user make a decision about the company being analyzed.

The steps involved in performing an informed analysis of a company include the following:

(1) Become familiar with the underlying economics of the company including both the range of activities the company engages in and the risks associated with those activities.

(2) Read the annual report including the auditors' opinion, the financial statements, and the notes to the financial statements. In doing so, uncertainties and large or unusual amounts or accounts can be identified and the details of specific elements in the financial statements can be reviewed.

(3) Perform time-series analysis and cross-sectional analysis using raw financial data, common size data, and ratio data as appropriate.

2. Understand the connection between prospective analysis and retro spective analysis. (pp. 593–594)

The analysis of financial statements is carried out because users need to make one or more decisions about the prospects of the firm being analyzed. Decision making is future oriented, therefore, the analysis should be future oriented as well. However, predicting future outcomes for a firm can be accomplished only by assessing the history of the firm. That is, we analyze the past (retrospective analysis) to see if we can identify factors or trends that will help us predict the future (prospective analysis).

Retrospective analysis can be carried out by examining the performance of a firm over several different periods (time-series analysis) and/or by comparing one firm to another (cross-sectional analysis). Cross-sectional analysis can be performed among firms within the same industry or among firms within different industries.

3. Be familiar with the types of data that are used in time-series analysis and cross-sectional analysis. (pp. 594–600)

Depending on the purpose of the analysis, three types of data can be used—raw financial data, common size data, and ratio data.

Raw financial data is the information that appears in the financial statements; for example, total sales on the income statement or total assets on the balance sheet. The financial statements usually present two or three years of comparative information while the annual report often contains a five to ten year summary of key financial data. Both are useful for time-series analysis.

Common size data is obtained by expressing each element within a financial statement as a percentage of some other element on that statement. For example, on the income statement each element is expressed as a percentage of sales; on the balance sheet each element is expressed as a percentage of total assets or total liabilities and shareholders' equity.

Learning Tip

For an example of a common size income statement see Exhibit 12-4 on page 600 of the text.

Common size financial statements are particularly useful in cross-sectional analysis because they allow for the comparison of firms of different size.

Ratio data are particularly useful because they provide information about the relationships between elements of the financial statements.

4. Be able to calculate and interpret the performance ratios. pp. 601–610)

The return on investment can be calculated from the perspective of different users. One such perspective is that of management; another is that of the owners, or shareholders, of the company. Management decides whether or not to acquire assets (the investment decision) and also decides how to finance the acquisition (the financing decision). The return on assets (ROA) is a measure of the return earned on the assets purchased by management. It is calculated as follows:

$$\text{ROA} = \frac{\text{Income before interest}}{\text{Average total assets}}$$

$$\text{ROA} = \frac{\text{Net inc.} + [\text{int. exp. x } (1 - \text{tax rate})]}{\text{Average total assets}}$$

Learning Tip

The income tax rate used in the calculation should be the sum of the marginal federal and provincial rates. As a practical matter, however, the average tax rate (income tax expense/earnings before taxes) is used most often.

Another way to calculate the ROA requires that the ratio be separated into its components—the profit margin ratio and the total asset turnover. It is calculated as follows:

$$\text{ROA} = \frac{\text{Net inc.} + [\text{int. exp. x } (1 - \text{tax rate})]}{\text{Sales revenue}} \text{ x } \frac{\text{Sales revenue}}{\text{Ave. total assets}}$$

or

ROA = profit margin ratio x total asset turnover

Learning Tip

Different strategies can lead to the same ROA. For example, a small profit margin with a high turnover or, conversely, a large profit margin with a low turnover can produce identical results.

The ROA is most useful for time-series analysis or for comparisons among firms in the same industry. Cross-sectional analysis across industries is not as useful because there are different risks inherent in the different types of assets employed in unrelated industries.

The owners, or shareholders, of the company will be more interested in the return on equity (ROE) ratio. It is calculated as follows:

$$\text{ROE} = \frac{\text{Net income} - \text{preferred dividends}}{\text{Average shareholders' equity}}$$

Learning Tip

Cross-sectional analysis of ROE across different industries is not recommended for the same reason as given for the ROA.

The financial leverage of a firm is a measure of the extent to which the company is financing its assets with debt rather than equity. A higher degree of financial leverage is advantageous if the after-tax rate of return on the assets of the firm is greater than the after-tax cost of the interest on the debt.

Learning Tip

Leverage does not provide unlimited advantage. As debt, and therefore financial leverage, increases lenders may perceive that the risk inherent in a firm is increasing and may charge a higher interest rate. When a firm's average borrowing costs exceed its ROA, it is no longer advantageous to finance with debt.

Theoretically, the optimum capital structure for a firm is at the point where ROE is maximized. See Exhibits 12-5 through 12-10 on pages 606-609 of the text.

Manufacturing firms also have to consider operating leverage which is a measure of their investment in production facilities. If the firm produces and sells a sufficient volume of goods, it will cover these fixed costs and earn a profit. However, if volume is not sufficient to cover the fixed costs, the firm will suffer significant losses.

5. Be able to calculate and interpret the turnover ratios. (pp. 610–614)

The turnover ratios provide some quantitative measures of the lead/lag relationships that exist among the cash flows connected with accounts receivable, inventory, and accounts payable.

The accounts receivable turnover ratio provides information about the credit granting and collection policies of a firm. It measures how often the old receivables are collected and replaced by new receivables. It is calculated as follows:

$$\text{A/R turnover} = \frac{\text{Sales on account}}{\text{Average accounts receivable}}$$

This ratio can be converted into a measure of the number of days that it takes to collect the average receivable as follows:

$$\text{Days to collect} = \frac{\text{365 days}}{\text{A/R turnover}}$$

Learning Tip

The number of days that it takes to collect the average accounts receivable can be compared to the receivable policy of the firm to determine how effectively the company is managing its receivables.

The A/R turnover and days to collect ratios can also be analysed on a time-series basis, to see how well a firm has managed its receivables over time, and on a cross-sectional basis, to see how it compares to its competitors.

The inventory turnover ratio measures how fast inventory is sold. It is determined as follows:

$$\text{Inventory turnover} = \frac{\text{Cost of goods sold}}{\text{Average inventory}}$$

The inventory turnover ratio can also be used to determine how long inventory is held prior to sale.

$$\text{Days inventory held} = \frac{365 \text{ days}}{\text{Inventory turnover}}$$

Learning Tip

For manufacturing firms, the days inventory held can be calculated separately for raw materials, work-in-process, and finished goods or it can be calculated for the inventory as a whole. For an example see page 612 of the text.

Both the turnover ratio and the days inventory held can be analyzed on a time-series basis and on a cross-sectional basis in order to measure the performance of the firm over time and in relation to its competition.

The accounts payable turnover measures how many times old accounts payable are paid off and new ones incurred. It is calculated as follows:

$$\text{A/P turnover} = \frac{\text{Credit Purchases}}{\text{Average accounts payable}}$$

As a practical matter, it is difficult to determine the amount of the credit purchases of a firm from the financial statements. As a result, the usual calculation is as follows:

$$\text{A/P turnover} = \frac{\text{Cost of goods sold}}{\text{Average accounts payable}}$$

Learning Tip

The alternative calculation is acceptable for retail firms, however, it is inappropriate for manufacturing firms. Cost of goods sold, for manufacturing firms, includes many production costs besides credit purchases of materials.

An alternative number for the numerator is "payments to suppliers" which could be taken from the statement of changes in financial position if the firm prepares the statement using the direct approach.

The A/P turnover can be converted to the number of days it takes to pay the average payable by the following formula:

$$\text{Days to pay} = \frac{\text{365 days}}{\text{Average A/P}}$$

Learning Tip

Both the turnover and the days to pay ratios can be used in both time-series analysis and cross-sectional analysis to compare performance across time and among competitors.

6. Be able to calculate and interpret the short-term liquidity ratios. (pp. 614–615)

Liquidity is a measure of the ability of the firm to convert its assets into cash in order to pay its liabilities. Two ratios that measure the liquidity of a firm are the current ratio and the quick ratio. The current ratio is calculated as follows:

$$\text{Current ratio} = \frac{\text{Current assets}}{\text{Current liabilities}}$$

Learning Tip

If the ratio is less than one, a firm has more current liabilities than current assets. If the ratio does not improve over time, the firm will almost certainly become insolvent. The general rule of thumb is that this ratio should be approximately equal to two.

This ratio is subject to manipulation at year end. A firm can improve its current ratio simply by paying off a portion of its current liabilities.

A stricter measure of the liquidity of a firm is the quick ratio. It is determined as follows:

$$\text{Quick ratio} = \frac{\text{Current assets} - \text{inventories}}{\text{Current liabilities}}$$

7. Be able to calculate and interpret the long-term liquidity ratios. (pp. 616–618)

Long-term liquidity refers to the ability of a firm to pay its long-term debt. Two ratios that are used to measure long-term liquidity are the debt/equity ratios and the times interest earned ratio.

The debt/equity ratios are a series of ratios that assess the magnitude of a firm's leverage. The first ratio measures the proportion of financing that comes from debt. It is calculated as follows:

$$D/E(I) = \frac{\text{Total liabilities}}{\text{Total liabilities + Shareholders' equity}}$$

The second ratio measures debt as a percentage of capital:

$$D/E(II) = \frac{\text{Total liabilities}}{\text{Total shareholders' equity}}$$

The third ratio measures long-term liabilities as a percentage of long-term financing. It is calculated as follows:

$$D/E(III) = \frac{\text{Total long-term liabilities}}{\text{Total long-term liabilities + shareholders' equity}}$$

Learning Tip

Each of these ratios must be compared over time (time-series analysis) and among competitive firms (cross-sectional analysis) in order to assess the relative long-term liquidity position of a firm. Remember that different industries have different acceptable liquidity positions.

8. Be familiar with the earnings per share ratio and the price/earnings ratio. (pp. 618–620)

The earnings per share (EPS) ratio is popular with the financial press and also with many investors. It has limited value, however, since it ignores the level of investment of the firm. In addition, the number of issued shares can differ significantly among firms. The basic formula is as follows:

$$\text{EPS} = \frac{\text{Net income} - \text{preferred dividends}}{\text{Weighted ave. no. of common shares}}$$

If a significant number of convertible securities exist (that is, securities that can be converted into common shares), GAAP requires that two EPS calculations be made—basic EPS and fully diluted EPS.

The fully diluted EPS ratio expands the denominator in the EPS ratio to include all convertible securities, assuming that they are dilutive, to produce the most conservative EPS figure. This number represents the worst case scenario.

Learning Tip

The EPS numbers are best used in time-series analysis. In addition, remember to exclude treasury shares from the denominator.

SELF STUDY

MATCHING

Match the key term to the best explanation.

Key Terms

A. Common size data
B. Common share equivalents
C Cross-sectional analysis
D Debt/equity ratios
E Leverage
F Operating leverage
G Optimal capital structure
H Profit margin ratio
I Prospective analysis
J Quick ratio
K Retrospective analysis
L Return on assets
M Return on equity
N Time-series analysis
O Total asset turnover

Explanations

1. __Analyzing financial data over several time periods.
2. __Analysis that attempts to project future results.
3. __Measures of a firm's leverage.
4. __The use of debt to improve the return to the shareholders.
5. __Can be split into the profit margin ratio and the total asset turnover ratio.
6. __Income statement data expressed as a percentage of sales revenue.
7. __An analysis based solely on historical data.
8. __An analysis comparing firms within the same industry.
9. __A theoretical point at which a firm's leverage will maximize the return to the owners.
10. __Compares the after-tax, but before-interest, earnings to the revenues of a firm.
11. __Measures the return on the investment made by the owners.
12. __The replacement of variable production costs with fixed production costs.
13. __Measures the amount of sales dollars generated per dollar of asset investment.
14. __Common shares that would be issued if convertible securities were exercised.
15. __A measure of a firm's short-term liquidity.

ASSESS YOUR RECALL

1. Identify the three categories of ratios that can be used in analyzing the performance of a firm and give one example for each category.

2. Identify the three types of data used in financial statement analysis and give an example for each type.

3. Identify and explain the two techniques used in retrospective analysis.

4. Identify each of the following ratios:

a. $\frac{\text{Current assets}}{\text{Current liabilities}}$ Current ratio

b. Profit margin ratio x Total asset turnover Return on asset

c. $\frac{\text{Net inc. + taxes + interest}}{\text{Interest}}$ TIE

d. $\frac{\text{Cost of goods sold}}{\text{Average inventory}}$ Inventory Turnover

e. $\frac{\text{Net inc.} - \text{preferred dividends}}{\text{Average owners' equity}}$ ROE

f. $\frac{\text{Total liabilities}}{\text{Owners' equity}}$ Debt/Equity

g. $\frac{\text{Cost of goods sold}}{\text{Average accounts payable}}$ A/P turnover

APPLYING YOUR KNOWLEDGE

1. The following data is taken from the December 31 financial statements of Poway, Inc. (amounts in thousands):

	19X4	19X3	19X2
Sales	$8,000	$7,300	$6,600
Interest expense	200	180	160
Net income	916	786.5	700
Preferred dividends	100	156.5	120
Total assets	4,400	4,000	3,700
Total liabilities	1,900	1,700	1,800
Total owners' equity	2,500	2,300	1,900
Tax rate	30%	30%	30%

For 19X4 and 19X3, calculate:

a. Return on assets (ROA), using the profit margin ratio and the total asset turnover.
b. Return on equity (ROE)
c. Comment on Poway's use of leverage.

2. The following data are taken from the December 31 financial statements of Larkin, Inc. (amounts in thousands):

	19X4	19X3	19X2
Sales	$56,250	$46,200	$35,900
Cost of goods sold	27,000	33,075	21,050
Accounts receivable	2,100	2,400	1,800
Inventory	1,500	3,000	4,350
Accounts payable	1,800	2,200	2,700

For 19X4 and 19X3, calculate:

a. Accounts receivable turnover and days to collect.
b. Inventory turnover and days inventory held.
c. Accounts payable turnover and days to pay.

3. Ramona, Inc. had the following financial results for three recent years (amounts in thousands):

	19X4	19X3	19X2
Cash	$ 600	$800	$400
Accounts receivable	2,600	2,400	3,200
Inventory	8,400	5,800	4,000
Other current assets	400	1,000	400
Noncurrent assets	60,000	50,000	40,000
Accounts payable	3,200	3,300	2,800
Taxes payable	1,600	1,980	1,600
Other current liabilities	1,200	660	600
Noncurrent liabilities	30,000	29,700	20,000

For all three years, calculate:

a. Current ratio
b. Quick ratio
c. Comment on the company's liquidity.

4. The following data was taken from the financial statements of Dulzura, Inc.'s (amounts in thousands):

	19X4	19X3	19X2
Sales	$47,880	$36,000	$23,760
Interest expense	810	600	420
Income tax expense	1,596	1,200	792
Net income	2,394	1,800	1,188
Current liabilities	4,500	2,850	2,250
Long-term liabilities	9,600	6,750	3,750
Owners' equity	12,000	9,000	6,000

For each of the three years, calculate:

a. Debt/equity ratios
   (1) D/E (I)
   (2) D/E (II)
   (3) D/E (III)
b. Times interest earned ratio

SOLUTIONS TO CHAPTER 12

MATCHING

1. N	6. A	11. M
2. I	7. K	12. F
3. D	8. C	13. O
4. E	9. G	14. B
5. L	10. H	15. J

ASSESS YOUR RECALL

1.

Performance:	return on equity, return on assets, leverage, inventory turnover, or accounts receivable turnover.
Short-term liquidity::	Current ratio or quick ratio.
Long-term liquidity:	Debt/equity ratios or times interest earned.

2.

Raw financial data:	any number from any of the financial statements. For example, sales or total assets.
Common size data:	one element of the income statement or balance sheet expressed as a percentage of another element on that statement. For example: net income as a percentage of sales, and current assets as a percentage of total assets.
Ratio data:	The comparison of one element on a financial statement to another element from the same statement or a different statement. For example: return on assets = income before interest/average total assets.

3. Retrospective analysis uses historical data to aid in the prediction of future performance. Historical data can be used to compare a firm's data over time (time-series analysis)or to compare one firm to another (cross-sectional analysis).

4. a. Current ratio
   b. Return on assets
   c. Times interest earned
   d. Inventory turnover
   e. Return on equity
   f. Debt/equity (II)
   g. Accounts payable turnover

APPLYING YOUR KNOWLEDGE

1. a.

$$\text{ROA} = \text{Profit margin ratio} \times \text{Total asset turnover}$$

$$= \frac{\text{Net inc.} + [\text{int. exp.} \times (1 - \text{TR})]}{\text{Sales revenue}} \times \frac{\text{Sales revenue}}{\text{Ave. tot. assets}}$$

$$19X4 = \frac{916 + [200 \times (1 - .30)]}{8{,}000} \times \frac{8{,}000}{(4{,}400 + 4{,}000)/2}$$

$$= .132 \times 1.905 = \underline{\underline{25.146\%}}$$

$$19X3 = \frac{786.5 + [180 \times (1 - .30)]}{7{,}300} \times \frac{7{,}300}{(4{,}000 + 3{,}700)/2}$$

$$= .125 \times 1.896 = \underline{\underline{23.7\%}}$$

b.

$$\text{ROE} = \frac{\text{Net income} - \text{preferred dividends}}{\text{Average owners' equity}}$$

$$19X4 = \frac{916 - 100}{(2{,}500 + 2{,}300)/2} = \frac{816}{2{,}400} = \underline{\underline{34\%}}$$

$$19X3 = \frac{786.5 - 156.5}{(2{,}300 + 1{,}900)/2} = \frac{630}{2{,}100} = \underline{\underline{30\%}}$$

c.

Since the ROE exceeds the ROA each year, the company is experiencing the advantage of positive leverage.

2. a.

	A/R Turnover	Days to Collect
	$\frac{\text{Credit sales}}{\text{Average A/R}}$	$\frac{365}{\text{A/R Turnover}}$
19X4:	$\frac{56{,}250}{(2{,}100 + 2{,}400)/2}$ = 25 times	$\frac{365}{25}$ = 14.6 days
19X3:	$\frac{46{,}200}{(2{,}400 + 1{,}800)/2}$ = 22 times	$\frac{365}{22}$ = 16.6 days

b.

Inv. Turnover	Days Held
$\frac{\text{Cost of goods sold}}{\text{Average inventory}}$	$\frac{365}{\text{Inv. Turnover}}$

19X4: $\frac{27{,}000}{(1{,}500 + 3{,}000)/2} = 12 \text{ times}$ $\frac{365}{12} = 30.4 \text{ days}$

19X3: $\frac{33{,}075}{(3{,}000 + 4{,}350)/2} = 9 \text{ times}$ $\frac{365}{9} = 40.6 \text{ days}$

c.

A/P Turnover	Days to Pay
$\frac{\text{Cost of goods sold}}{\text{Average A/P}}$	$\frac{365}{\text{A/P Turnover}}$

19X4: $\frac{27{,}000}{(1{,}800 + 2{,}200)/2} = 13.5 \text{ times}$ $\frac{365}{13.5} = 27.04 \text{ days}$

19X3: $\frac{33{,}075}{(2{,}200 + 2{,}700)/2} = 13.5 \text{ times}$ $\frac{365}{13.5} = 27.04 \text{ days}$

3. a.

Current Ratio	Quick Ratio
$\frac{\text{Current assets}}{\text{Current liabilities}}$	$\frac{\text{Current assets} - \text{Inventory}}{\text{Current liabilities}}$

19X4: $\frac{12{,}000}{6{,}000} = 2.0$ $\frac{12{,}000 - 8{,}400}{6{,}000} = 0.60$

19X3: $\frac{10{,}000}{5{,}940} = 1.68$ $\frac{10{,}000 - 5{,}800}{5{,}940} = 0.71$

19X3: $\frac{8,000}{5,000} = 1.60$ $\frac{8,000-4,000}{5,000} = 0.80$

c.

The current ratio appears to have improved over the period: however, as seen from the quick ratio, this improvement is due primarily to increasing inventory balances.

4.

	D/E (I)		D/E (II)	
	$\frac{\text{Total Liabilities}}{\text{Tot. Liabl. + S.E.}}$		$\frac{\text{Total Liabilities}}{\text{Shareholders' Eq.}}$	
19X4:	$\frac{4,500 + 9,600}{4,500 + 9,600 + 12,000}$	= 54.02%	$\frac{14,100}{12,000}$	= 117.5 %
19X3:	$\frac{2,850 + 6,750}{2,850 + 6,750 + 9,000}$	= 51.6 %	$\frac{9,600}{9,000}$	= 106.7 %
19X2:	$\frac{2,250 + 3,750}{2,250 + 3,750 + 6,000}$	= 50 %	$\frac{6,000}{6,000}$	= 100 %

	D/E (III)		b. TIE	
	$\frac{\text{Total L-T Liabilities}}{\text{Tot. L-T Liabl. + S.E.}}$		$\frac{\text{NI + Tax + Int}}{\text{Interest}}$	
19X4:	$\frac{9,600}{9,600 + 12,000}$	= 44.44%	$\frac{2,394 + 1,596 + 810}{810}$	= 5.9 times
19X3:	$\frac{6,750}{6,750 + 9,000}$	= 42.86%	$\frac{1,800 + 1,200 + 600}{600}$	= 6.0 times
19X2:	$\frac{3,750}{3,750 + 6,000}$	= 38.46%	$\frac{1,188 + 792 + 420}{420}$	=5.7 times

CHAPTER 13

COMPLEX ORGANIZATIONS

CHAPTER OVERVIEW

This final chapter outlines the types of complex organizations that can result when one firm acquires an ownership interest in another firm. The issues surrounding complex intercorporate investments include valuation decisions, accounting procedures, and the consolidation of financial statements. All of these issues are raised and discussed in the chapter.

A firm may decide to invest in the voting shares of another company for a number of reasons:

- it may have excess cash that is available to use as a passive, short-term or long-term investment;
- it may wish to gain influence or control over a competitor (horizontal integration) or a supplier or customer (vertical integration); or
- it may wish to smooth out cyclical fluctuations in its operating cycle (diversification).

Influence or control can be obtained either by buying the assets of the other firm or by buying its issued capital shares. The purchasing company can make the acquisition by paying cash, by assuming debt, by giving some of its own shares, or by some combination of the three.

When a firm acquires more than 50% of another firm's voting shares, the investor must prepare financial statements which consolidate the accounts of the investor company with those of the investee company. On its own books, the investor company records the transactions related to the investment using the equity method. The adjustment to a consolidated basis is made at each year end. Depending on the circumstances, the consolidation may be valued under either the purchase method or the pooling of interests method. In Canada, the pooling of interests method is rarely used.

Both the investor and the investee have separate sets of accounting records. The consolidation process is accomplished by using a worksheet and a set of consolidation entries. None of the consolidation entries is recorded in either set of accounting records. The completed worksheet provides the accounts and amounts to be used in preparing the consolidated financial statements.

If the investor company owns less than 100% of the voting shares of the investee company, the noncontrolling shareholders, called the minority interest, must also be reflected on the consolidated statements.

LEARNING OBJECTIVES

1. Be familiar with the reasons for, and the methods of, acquiring influence or control over another company.
2. Understand the valuation issues at the date of acquisition.
3. Understand the income and dividend recognition issues subsequent to acquisition.
4. Be familiar with the consolidation procedures required where the investor owns 100% of the shares of the investee.
5. Be aware of the consolidation procedures where a minority interest exists.
6. Be aware of the effects that consolidation has on financial statement analysis.

CHAPTER REVIEW

1. Be familiar with the reasons for, and the methods of, acquiring influence or control over another firm. (pp. 659–661)

A firm will invest in another firm to increase income; to gain significant influence or control over a competitor, a supplier, or a customer; or to protect itself from cyclical fluctuations in its operating cycle.

Significant influence or control can be obtained either by acquiring the assets of the other firm or by buying its voting shares. An investor is considered to have significant influence over an investee if it owns 20% to 50% of the voting shares of the investee and if it is able to influence the operating, investing, and financing decisions of the investee. An investor has control over an investee if it owns more than 50% of the voting shares of the investee. The purchasing company can make the acquisistion by paying cash, by trading shares for shares, by assuming debt in exchange for shares, or by some combination of the three.

In a share acquisition the acquired firm, the investee, remains a separate legal, taxable, and accounting entity.

2. Understand the valuation issues at the date of acquisition. (pp. 661–666)

If the investor company acquires only the assets of the investee, the assets must be recorded on the books of the acquiring company at the historical, or acquisition, cost.

If the assets of the investee are acquired for cash, the cash paid is the measure of acquisition cost. The acquisition cost must be allocated among the assets based on their fair market values relative to the cost; that is, like a basket purchase. If the assets are acquired by the assumption of debt, acquisition cost is equal to the net present value of the debt at the date of issuance. If, on the other hand, the investor company acquires the shares (not the assets) of the investee company, the investment is recorded at its acquisition cost in an account called something similar to "Investment in X Company".

Learning Tip

The method described above, the purchase method, is used to record the transaction when the investor pays cash or issues debt in exchange for the shares of the investee. It is also used in transactions involving share swaps that do not qualify as pooling of interests.

The net assets acquired are recorded at their fair market values. This would include recognition of assets that may not be reflected on the books of the investee; for example, intangible assets that were developed internally. In addition, if the purchase price exceeds the fair market value of the net assets acquired, the difference is recognized as goodwill.

Learning Tip

Any income earned by the investee during the current period and prior to the date of acquisition, is not recognized by the investor. As a result the retained earnings account of the investee is not combined with that of the investor on consolidation. The retained earnings and the common share accounts on the books of the investee are eliminated against the investment account on the books of the investor.

If the acquisition consists of a 100% share-for-share swap, and it is not possible to identify the acquirer, or parent company, the transaction may be accounted for as a pooling of interests. A pooling of interests is not viewed in the same way as a purchase; instead it is considered to be the combination of two entities. As a result, the net assets acquired are recorded at their old book values.

Learning Tip

Under the pooling of interests method, the two firms are assumed to have been combined forever. As a result, the income earned by the parties to the transaction in the current period is combined on consolidation. The retained earnings accounts of both companies are also combined on the consolidated balance sheet. The pooling of interests method is rarely used for intercorporate investments in Canada because GAAP allows it only when the acquirer cannot be identified.

3. Understand the income and dividend recognition issues subsequent to acquisition. (pp. 666–671)

After acquisition, the assets of both corporations are accounted for in the usual way in their own separate accounting records. Capital tangible and intangible assets are amortized over their remaining useful lives, prepaid assets are expensed as they are used, and inventory is expensed through cost of goods sold when it is sold.

Share acquisitions are accounted for using the cost method if the investor owns less than 20% of the voting shares; using the equity method if the investor owns between 20%-50% of the shares and can exercise significant influence; and by the consolidation method if the investor owns more than 50% of the voting shares. Under the cost method used for long-term, passive (or portfolio) investments, the shares are written down to market following the LCM rule only if the shares have suffered a permanent decline in value. For short-term, passive investments (temporary investments), the LCM rule is applied at the end of every fiscal year. The LCM method was discussed in chapter 6.

Under the cost method for long-term portfolio investments, interest and dividends received on the holdings are credited to revenue accounts.

The equity method requires that the investor account for its ownership interest in the investee in an investment account. The investment account initially reflects the cost of the acquisition. It is subsequently adjusted to recognize the investor's post-acquisition share of the investee's net income/loss and for the investors share of dividends declared by the investee. Net income increases the account, while net losses and declared dividends reduce it. The journal entries to reflect net income and dividends received are as follows:

A—Investment in shares	XX	
SE—Equity in earnings of investment		XX
A—Cash	XX	
A—Investment in shares		XX

Learning Tip

For a numeric example see the box on page 670 of the text.

Remember, if the purchase method is used, the acquired net assets will be included in the investment account at their fair market value. If the fair market value of the capital assets exceeds their book value, the difference between book value and fair value is also included in the investment account and must be amortized over the remaining useful lives of the acquired assets. If the purchase price exceeds the total fair market value of the net assets acquired, goodwill will also be included in the investment account and must be amortized over its useful life as well. The amortization of the excess of fair value over book value will reduce both the investment account balance and the amount of the investee net income recorded by the investor. The entry to record these additional expenses is as follows:

SE—Equity in earnings of investment	XX	
A—Investment in shares		XX

4. Be familiar with the consolidation procedures required where the investor owns 100% of the shares of the investee. (pp. 671–679)

At the date of acquisition the investor company (parent) records the purchase in an investment account. This account, under the equity method, will then be adjusted to reflect the parent's interest in the subsidiary company. At the end of each accounting period, the separate financial statements of the two firms are combined on a worksheet using a series of consolidation worksheet entries.

Learning Tip

These are not journal entries. They are not recorded on the books of either firm. They appear only on the worksheet.

The purpose of these entries is to ensure that the consolidated financial statements reflect both the combined assets and liabilities of the companies at their proper values and the combined revenues and expenses of the companies (adjusted for any intercompany transactions). The worksheet consists of the trial balance of each company, the consolidation elimination and adjusting entries, and the consolidated totals. The consolidation entries consist of the following:

(1) To reverse the current year's earnings and dividends reflected in the investment account:

SE—Equity in earnings of investment	XX	
SE—Dividends declared		XX
A—Investment in Subsidiary		XX

(2) To eliminate the investment account of the parent and the shareholders' equity accounts of the subsidiary, and to recognize any excess of the fair market value over the book value of assets acquired as well as goodwill if it has also been purchased:

SE—Shareholders' equity (Sub)	XX	
A—Property, plant and equipment	XX	
A—Goodwill	XX	
A—Investment in Subsidiary		XX

(3) To recognize any additional amortization on the excess fair market value of capital assets and to amortize goodwill if it has been purchased.

SE—Amortization expense	XX	
SE—Amortization expense	XX	
XA—Accumulated amortization		XX
A—Goodwill		XX

(4) To eliminate any intercompany transactions; for example, intercompany purchases, sales, payables, and receivables.

L—Accounts payable	XX	
A—Accounts receivable		XX
SE—Sales	XX	
SE—Cost of goods sold		XX

Learning Tip

For a numeric example see the box on page 678 of the text and Exhibit 13-10 on page 679.

When the worksheet is completed and balanced, the consolidated financial statements can be prepared directly from it.

Learning Tip

Under the equity method, consolidated net income and retained earnings will be equal to the net income and retained earnings of the parent company.

5. Be aware of the consolidated procedures where a minority interest exists. (pp. 679–681)

When the investor company does not own 100% of the voting shares of the investee company the other, non-controlling, shareholders are referred to as the minority interest. The portion of the net assets belonging to the minority interest is shown on the consolidated balance sheet as the final element in the liability section. Similarly, the minority interest share of subsidiary net income is shown as a reduction to net income on the consolidated income statement

Learning Tip

Most companies disclose the minority interest on the consolidated balance sheet between the liability section and the shareholders' equity section.

For a numeric example see Exhibits 13-11 and 13-12 on pages 680 and 682 of the text.

6. Be aware of the effects that consolidation has on financial statement analysis. (pp. 680–682)

Under the equity method, the investor's interest in the investee are summarized in the Investment in Shares account and the Equity in Earnings of Investment account. However, when an investor consolidates its financial statements with those of the investee, detailed information about the investee's assets and liabilities is not disclosed.

The appearance of the consolidated financial statements is significantly different from that of a parent company using the equity method. The individual amounts of assets and liabilities reported on the consolidated balance sheet are different from the amounts that would be shown under the equity method. However, net income and shareholders' equity amounts are the same under both methods. Consequently, the return on equity ratio calculation yields the same results under both methods.

The ratios that will be affected are those that use asset and liability balances in the calculation; for example, the debt/equity ratio, the return on assets ratio, the turnover ratios, the current ratio, and the quick ratio.

SELF STUDY

MATCHING

Match the key term to the best explanation.

Key Terms

A. Consolidation
B. Controlling interest
C. Diversification
D. Excess fair market value
E. Horizontal integration
F. Investee
G. Investor
H. Minority interest
I. Parent company
J. Passive investment
K. Pooling of interests
L. Purchase method
M. Cost method
N. Equity method
O. Subsidiary

Explanations

1. ___ A company that acquires the shares of another company as an investment.
2. ___ Used in acquisitions involving a share swap where the acquirer cannot be identified.
3. ___ What a company is called if another firm owns more than 50% of its voting shares.
4. ___ Used when the acquisition of the net assets of a company is recorded at the cost to the acquiring company.
5. ___ Required of firms that own more than 50% of the voting shares of another company.
6. ___ The difference between the fair market value and book value of a subsidiary's net assets at the date of acquisition.
7. ___ When the number of shares held by an investor is not large enough to provide the investor with any control or influence.
8. ___ A synonym for non-controlling interest.
9. ___ Method of accounting for an investee when the investor can exercise significant influence over the investee.
10. ___ Usually means ownership of more than 50% of another firm's voting shares.
11. ___ When one firm buys a competitor firm in order to increase its own market share.
12. ___ Method of accounting for a long-term passive investment.
13. ___ The acquisition of companies that are counter-cyclical to yours.
14. ___ A company whose shares are acquired by another company.
15. ___ A company that owns more than 50% of the common shares of another company.

ASSESS YOUR RECALL

1. Explain the difference among a passive investment, an investment subject to significant influence, and an investment subject to control. Identify the appropriate accounting method used to record each.

2. If a parent company acquires a subsidiary company for a price that exceeds the book value of the net assets of the subsidiary, how is the difference treated in a consolidation?

3. Explain why consolidated net income is identical to the net income reported using the equity method.

4. Explain why net income using the pooling of interests method is usually higher than net income using the purchase method.

5. Explain why the net assets are valued at their fair market values under the purchase method and at their book values under the pooling of interests method.

6. What three basic consolidation worksheet entries are made a year after acquisition when the parent company uses the equity method to account for its investment in the subsidiary?

APPLYING YOUR KNOWLEDGE

1. On January 1, 19X3, Parker Corporation acquired 100% of the voting common shares of Subica, Inc. for $750,000. The book value of Subica's net assets was $600,000. Assume that the fair market value of the capital assets exceeded their book value by $50,000 on the date of acquisition. During the year, Subica earned $120,000 and paid $20,000 in dividends. Parker uses straight-line amortization and the equity method. The remaining useful life of the assets acquired is 10 years with no residual value. Any goodwill acquired is amortized over 20 years.

   a. Prepare any journal entries necessary to record Parker's investment and the subsequent activity.
   b. Prepare the consolidation worksheet entries at year end.

2. Crown, Inc. and Day Corporation agree to merge, by Crown issuing 8,000 shares (market value $240,000) in exchange for all of Day's common shares. The difference between the market value of Crown's shares and the book value of Day's net assets includes $40,000 of excess fair market value on Day's noncurrent assets. Both companies remain separate legal entities. Their respective balance sheets as of December 31, 19X3 were:

	Crown, Inc.	Day Corp.
Assets:		
Current assets	$280,000	$ 55,000
Noncurrent assets	270,000	80,000
Totals	$550,000	$135,000
Liabilities & Owners' Equity:		
Liabilities	$140,000	$ 60,000
Common shares	365,000	55,000
Retained earnings	45,000	20,000
Totals	$550,000	$135,000

Net income for the year: Crown, $40,000; Day, $10,000.

a. Prepare the journal entry on Crown's books to record its investment in Day assuming that the transaction is accounted for as a purchase.

b. Prepare the consolidation worksheet under the same assumption.

Purchase Method

Account	Crown*		Day		Consolidating Entries		Consolidated Totals	
	Debit	Credit	Debit	Credit	Debit	Credit	Debit	Credit
Current assets								
Investment in Day								
Noncurrent assets								
Goodwill								
Liabilities								
Common stock								
Contributed capital								
Retained earnings								
Totals								

* Reflects investment entry

3. On January 1, 19X5, Valdez, Inc. acquired 70% of the common shares of Johnson Corporation for $500,000. At the date of acquisition, the shareholders' equity accounts of Johnson had the following balances.

Common shares	$250,000
Contributed capital	150,000
Retained earnings	100,000
Total	$500,000

Excess fair market value of $50,000 exists on Johnson's capital assets. Valdez uses straight-line amortization assuming a 10-year useful life and no residual value. Any goodwill is amortized over 20 years. The income statements and balance sheets for the two companies for the year ending December 31, 19X5 were as follows:

	Valdez	Johnson
Sales	$ 500,000	$ 300,000
Cost of goods sold	(275,000)	(175,000)
Amortization	(135,000)	(25,000)
Equity in Johnson's earnings	60,000	
Net income	$ 150,000	$ 100,000
Dividends declared	$ 125,000	$ 75,000
Current assets	$ 312,500	$302,500
Investment in Johnson	507,500	
Noncurrent assets	430,000	372,500
Total assets	$ 1,250,000	$ 675,000
Current liabilities	$ 197,500	$ 100,000
Noncurrent liabilities	52,500	50,000
Common shares	500,000	250,000
Contributed capital	250,000	150,000
Retained earnings	250,000	125,000
Total liabilities and shareholders' equity	$ 1,250,000	$ 675,000

$60,000 of Valdez' current liabilities is payable to Johnson.

a. Reconstruct the journal entries that were posted to the investment account on Valdez' books assuming that the equity method was used.
b. Prepare a consolidated worksheet at December 31, 19X5.

SOLUTIONS TO CHAPTER 13

MATCHING

1. G	6. D	11. E
2. K	7. J	12. M
3. O	8. H	13. C
4. L	9. N	14. F
5. A	10. B	15. I

ASSESS YOUR RECALL

1. When one firm owns less than 20% of common shares of another company, it is considered to be a passive investment. An investment of this size does not allow the investor to exercise any influence or control over the investee. The appropriate accounting method to use is the cost method. If an individual investment in the portfolio is considered to have suffered a permanent decline in value, the investment should be written down. Subsequent recovery of the write-down is not permitted.

When one firm owns 20%–50% of the voting shares of another company and is able to exercise significant influence over the operating, investing, and financing decisions of the investee, the appropriate accounting method to use is the equity method.

When one company owns more than 50% of the voting shares of another company, the investor has a controlling interest. The investor must prepare consolidated financial statements.

2. The difference, called excess fair value, results from the fact that the fair market value of assets acquired exceeds their book value at the date of acquisition and/or from the fact that the acquiring company has paid for goodwill. The excess fair value is reflected in the consolidated financial statements as increases in the reported amounts for capital assets and/or goodwill (on the balalnce sheet) and as an increase in amortization expense (on the income statement).

3. The equity method is often referred to as a one-line consolidation method because the balance sheet effects of consolidation are captured in the account called Investment in Subsidiary and the income statement effects are captured in the account called Equity in Earnings of Subsidiary.

Under consolidation, the investment account is eliminated and the assets, liabilities, revenues, and expenses of the two companies are combined on a line-by-basis.

4. Under the purchase method net assets are recorded at their fair market values which are usually higher than their old book values. As a result, amortization and other expenses will usually be higher under the purchase method. In addition,

under the pooling of interests method, the investor can recognize all of the investee's income arising in the year of acquisition.

5. Fair market values are used under the purchase method because the acquisition is viewed as a purchase of the net assets of the investee. Asset purchases are recorded at historical cost which is the price paid to acquire them; that is, their fair market value at the date of acquisition.

Book values are used in the pooling of interests method because the acquisition is viewed not as a purchase but as a combination of the two firms where the identity of the acquirer cannot be determined. As a result, there is no need to change the valuation basis of the assets of either company.

6. The three basic consolidation worksheet entries are: (1) reverse the current year's income and dividends from the investment account; (2) eliminate the investment account and the subsidiary's shareholders' equity accounts and at the same time recognize any increases in assets or goodwill; (3) amortize any goodwill and any increases attributable to tangible capital assets.

APPLYING YOUR KNOWLEDGE

1.

a. To record Parker's acquisition of Subica:

A—Investment in Subica	750,000	
A—Cash		750,000

To record Parker's equity in Subica's income:

A—Investment in Subica	120,000	
SE—Equity in Subica's Earnings		120,000

To record receipt of Subica's dividends:

A—Cash	20,000	
A—Investment in Subica		20,000

To record the additional amortization expense:

SE—Equity in Subica's Earnings	10,000	
A—Investment in Subica		10,000

Amortization of capital assets = 50,000/10 years = 5,000
Amortization = 750,000 − 600,000 = 150,000 − 50,000 =
= 100,000/20 years = 5,000

b. Consolidating worksheet entries

To reverse Subica's 19X3 income and dividends:

SE—Equity in Subica's Earnings	110,000	
SE—Declared Dividends		20,000
A—Investment in Subica		90,000

To eliminate the investment account & Subica's shareholders' equity:

SE—Shareholders' Equity (Subica)	600,000	
A—Capital Assets	50,000	
A—Goodwill	100,000	
A—Investment in Subica		750,000

To recognize additional amortization expense:

SE—Amortization Expense	5,000	
SE—Amortization Expense	5,000	
XA—Accumulated Amortization		5,000
A—Goodwill		5,000

2.

a.

A—Investment in Day	240,000	
SE—Common Shares (Crown)		240,000

3.

a. To record the investment:

A—Investment in Johnson	500,000	
A—Cash		500,000

To record Valdez' share of Johnson's income:

A—Investment in Johnson	70,000	
OE—Equity in Johnson's Earnings		70,000

* 70% x 100,000 = 70,000

To record Valdez' share of Johnson's dividends:

A—Cash	52,500	
A—Investment in Johnson		52,500

* 70% x 75,000 = 52,500

To record the additional amortization expense:

SE—Equity in Johnson's Earnings	10,000	
A—Investment in Johnson		10,000

* Amortization = 50,000/10 years = 5,000
Amortization = 100,000/20 years = 5,000

b. Explanations for consolidating worksheet entries:

(a) Reversal of Johnson's 19X5 income & dividends.
(b) Elimination of the investment account.
(c) Recognizing goodwill amortization.
(d) Recognizing additional amortization on capital assets.
(e) Establishing minority interest in Johnson's 19X5 income.
(f) Elimination of intercompany payable and receivable.

Purchase Method

Account	Crown*		Day		Consolidating Entries		Consolidated Totals	
	Debit	Credit	Debit	Credit	Debit	Credit	Debit	Credit
Current assets	280,000		55,000				335,000	
Investment in Day	240,000					(a) 240,000		
Noncurrent assets	270,000		80,000		(a) 40,000		390,000	
Goodwill					(a) 125,000		125,000	
Liabilities		140,000		60,000				200,000
Common shares		605,000		50,000	(a) 55,000		605,000	
Retained earnings		45,000		20,000	(a) 20,000		45,000	
Totals	790,000	790,000	135,000	135,000	240,000	240,000	850,000	850,000

* Reflects investment entry

Account	Valdez Debit	Valdez Credit	Johnson Debit	Johnson Credit	Consolidating Entries Debit	Consolidating Entries Credit	Consolidated Totals Debit	Consolidated Totals Credit
Current assets	312,500		302,500			(f) 60,000	555,000	
Investment in Johnson	507,500					(a) 7,500		
						(b) 500,000		
Noncurrent assets	430,000		372,500		(b) 50,000	(d) 5,000	847,500	
Goodwill					(b) 100,000	(c) 5,000	95,000	
Liabilities		250,000		150,000	(f) 60,000			340,000
Common shares		500,000		250,000	(b) 250,000			500,000
Contributed capital		250,000		150,000	(b) 150,000			250,000
Retained earnings*		225,000		100,000	(b) 100,000			225,000
Minority interest					(a) 22,500	(b) 150,000		
						(e) 30,000		157,500
Sales		500,000		300,000				800,000
Cost of goods sold	275,000		175,000				450,000	
Amortiz. expense	135,000		25,000		(d) 5,000		165,000	
Amort. exp.					(c) 5,000		5,000	
Equity in Johnson's earnings		60,000			(a) 60,000			
Minority interest in net income					(e) 30,000		30,000	
Dividends declared	125,000		75,000			(a) 75,000	125,000	
Totals	1,785,000	1,785,000	950,000	950,000	832,500	832,500	2,272,500	2,272,500

* January 1, 19X5 balances